Praise for *Don't Make It Look Self-Published*

As the CEO of a book publicity firm, I've seen it all: books with brilliant content that get overlooked simply because the design falls flat. In *Don't Make It Look Self-Published*, George Stevens delivers what every indie author needs: a clear, engaging, and genuinely helpful guide to making your book look as good as it reads. With warmth, wit, and deep expertise, George shows that great design isn't about vanity; it's about credibility. This book is both a practical resource and a confidence boost for any author ready to put their best book forward.

Sandra Poirier Smith
CEO, Smith Publicity, Inc.

George nailed it with this book. It's the straight talk indie authors desperately need before diving into the design process—smart, grounded, and refreshingly free of fluff. If you're serious about your book not looking like amateur hour, this should be required reading. He breaks down how to find the right designer, what to expect from the process, and why cheap shortcuts almost always backfire. It's not just about getting a good-looking book—it's about building a professional collaboration that respects your message. Every indie author should read this before they hit "publish." Honestly, if I could mail this to half the clients who've come to me after a Canva catastrophe or a bargain-bin disaster, I would. *Don't Make it Look Self-Published* is preventive medicine for every indie author's regret.

Ian Koviak
*the*BookDesigners

A good book is a product that must put its best face forward in a crowded market—and George B. Stevens, master book designer, understands that better than anyone. Now, with *Don't Make It Look Self-Published*, he shares that wisdom with indie authors everywhere. This is the definitive guide to the most misunderstood phase of book publishing: book design. With clarity, wit, humor, and deep empathy for the authors he serves, Stevens reveals what great designers actually do—and what authors must do to find and collaborate with them. As an author of commercially successful books and the founder of a publishing company that has served hundreds of authors, I can say this with confidence: the insights in *Don't Make It Look Self-Published* can make the difference between launching a book that opens doors and one that quietly disappears. Stevens gives authors the language, the leverage, and the confidence to demand better. This isn't just a book—it's a game plan for serious authors who want to be taken seriously. Book coaches, editors, strategists, and publicists should gift it to their clients. And anyone working in publishing would be smart to keep it within arm's reach.

Kate Colbert
Author of *Think Like a Marketer* and *Commencement*,
Founder and President of Silver Tree Publishing

I've had the privilege of working closely with George on both of my books, from cover design and publishing advice to final formatting. He's not just a talented designer; he's a true partner who understands what it takes to make a self-published book look professional and feel like you. *Don't Make It Look Self-Published* is exactly what you'd expect from George: clear, practical, encouraging, and a must-have for any author.

Anthony Damaschino
Author of *The Empty Nest Blueprint* books

In *Don't Make It Look Self-Published*, George Stevens shares his knowledge of and passion for top-notch book design. He reveals the secrets to finding the right designer and collaborating well with them. With this book, you'll be prepared to put together a thoughtful cover brief, provide meaningful feedback, and much more. Highly recommend for indie authors who want to publish a high-quality, professional book.

Jenny Lisk

Nonfiction publishing and marketing strategist and author of *Future Widow*

A total gem for indie authors! This book will guide you to create a standout reader experience, smooth out your publishing process (aka reduce your stress!), and position you to boost book sales with confidence. Having partnered with George on both my own book and those of my coaching clients, I can say firsthand: his design insights and communication style truly elevate every project.

Lanette Pottle

Bestselling book coach and author of *Profit Write: How to Create Books that Grow Your Business, Brand, and Impact*

You've heard it said, 'Don't judge a book by its cover'—but the cover is the brand identity of the book! That's why George Stevens is a game-changer for indie authors. Working with him is a joy, and this book is packed with the same genius, clarity, and care he brings to every project. A must-read for authors everywhere who want their book to look as good as it reads.

Allison Trowbridge

Author and founder/CEO of Copper Books

FIND YOUR DREAM DESIGNER!
COLLABORATE WITH CONFIDENCE!

DON'T
MAKE IT
LOOK
SELF
PUBLISHED

THE INDIE AUTHOR'S GUIDE TO
BOOK DESIGN

GEORGE B. STEVENS
WITH A FOREWORD BY STEVE SPANGLER

Olinova
Press

Don't Make It Look Self-Published:
The Indie Author's Guide to Book Design

Copyright 2025 © George B. Stevens
Foreword copyright 2025 © Steve Spangler

Olinova
Press

Published by Olinova Press
North Charleston, SC

Edited by Nate Best
Cover design and typesetting by G Sharp Design, LLC
Proofreading by LKM Editorial, LLC
Author photo by Melissa Toms

First edition, August 2025

Paperback ISBN: 979-8-9992868-0-2
Library of Congress Control Number: 2025913512

Created in the United States of America

To Sarah and Hazel.

CONTENTS

FOREWORD

BY STEVE SPANGLER

Emmy Award Winner and Bestselling Author of
The Engagement Effect

Ask any author what it takes to write a great book, and you'll hear about discipline, deadlines, structure, voice, and vision.

What you don't hear as often—but should—is design.

In the world of independent publishing, too many authors treat design like a footnote. They've worked so hard to get the content right that by the time the manuscript is finished, they're out of creative energy—and out of budget. The design becomes an afterthought, something to check off the list. And that's the moment when great ideas get quietly buried behind covers that scream, "I made this myself".

That disconnect is what George Stevens tackles head-on in this book.

George doesn't waste time defending fonts or preaching aesthetic trends. This isn't a book about design theory—it's a book about authorship. About credibility. About what it means to not only write a book worth reading but to package it in a way that respects the work, elevates the message, and earns the reader's trust before a single page is turned.

In these pages, George reframes what design really is: not a product, but a process. A process rooted in thoughtful collaboration, creative clarity, and a deep respect for the author's voice and vision. He challenges the myth that only traditionally published books can look polished and powerful. He shows how the right approach to design isn't about vanity—it's about value. Because when a book looks like it matters, people treat it like it matters.

> **The right approach to design isn't about vanity—it's about value. When a book looks like it matters, people treat it like it matters.**

I had the opportunity to work with George on the cover of my most recent book, *The Engagement Effect*, and I saw firsthand how deeply he understands both the art and the strategy of great book design. It was clear to me then—just as it will be clear to you now—that George is doing more than design work. He's helping authors show up in the world the way they were meant to be seen.

What makes this guide essential isn't just George's experience—it's his empathy. He's sat at the crossroads of content and design long enough to understand what most authors are really asking when they say, "Just don't make it look self-published." They're asking: *Will my book be taken seriously? Will my message connect? Will my work be judged before it's even read?*

This book is George's answer to those questions. It's a resource for every author who understands that writing the book is only half the journey—and that the rest of the path requires just as much intentionality, just as much craft, and just as much courage.

Turn the page. The rest of your book begins here.

Steve Spangler
Author of *The Engagement Effect*
Member, National Speakers Association Hall of Fame
Two-time Emmy Award Winner

THE AUTHOR ONION

This is not a book about graphic design.

At no point will I subject you to my preferred Photoshop techniques, nor bore you with esoteric design philosophy. You shall not endure a hagiographical overview of celebrated book designers. There shall be no passionate defense of Helvetica.[1]

At its core, this is a book about modern authorship. It's a book for the brave souls who willfully swan dive into the self-publishing frying pan. After all, no one is *forcing* you to assume the lofty burdens of the independent author. The effort, the expense, the exposure to criticism: you don't have to deal with any of it. Yet you heed the call. Publishing your book will stitch a layer of complexity onto your very existence; yet you are compelled by a greater purpose.

In this way, publishing a book is a lot like becoming a parent. Reread the previous paragraph, swapping "author" with "parent" and "publishing a book" with "having a kid." It reads almost seamlessly.

---

1 For the record, I do love Helvetica.

Parenting vis-a-vis Authoring

"Parenting is difficult!"

This is not a carefully guarded secret. When my wife and I were expecting our daughter in 2020, our parent-friends barraged us with playful warnings about our impending new reality. We heard all the classics:

"Get your sleep now!"

"Hope you like 'Wheels On the Bus'!"

"Having a kid is the best mistake you'll ever make!"

But by far, the most common refrain was:

"It's hard, but it's worth it!"

Hard but worth it. Intuitively, this seemed accurate. But prior to my daughter's arrival, I didn't grasp its true meaning. Having no childcare experience, my understanding of parental rigors was based on spot public observations like witnessing a dad tearing through a playground in pursuit of a loose-cannon toddler or a mother on an airplane, hushing her squealing baby amidst a gauntlet of eyerolls and glares from unsympathetic nonparents like me.

Shoot, even changing a dirty diaper seemed like a Herculean task back then. It was these scenes, and many like them, that my kidless mind conjured when I heard the words, "Parenting is hard."

Then I became a parent and realized I had it all wrong.

Those momentary flaps—the dad chasing the toddler, the mom in the airplane—are no big deal. They're unenduring inconveniences that represent a few of the many ephemeral fires a parent will douse on a daily basis. They're blips on the radar; you deal with them and move on.

So what *really* makes parenting hard? It's those moments that test you at your most vulnerable state, when your inner voice is clamoring for measures of rest and self-care that were plentiful in your previous, unencumbered life. Now, parental instincts force you to marginalize both.

> "Hard" is peeling yourself out of bed when the baby monitor issues an ear-splitting wail, mere seconds after you've *finally* melted into a deep sleep.

> "Hard" is watching your panicking one-year-old get chest X-rays amidst a four-hour ER visit.

> "Hard" is the Sisyphean drudgery of piecing your house back together each evening, knowing it shall be dismantled again the next day by tiny, exploring hands.

To take it one step further: what's really "hard" is the *aggregate* of all these demanding moments, which are constant and unyielding. They layer together to form a monstrous onion, branded with the words "*Your New Life as a Parent.*" You don't always think about the individual layers, but you can point at the onion and say, "*That. That's what's hard.*" (And—yes—it's worth it.)

> **What's really "hard" is the aggregate of all these demanding moments, which are constant and unyielding.**

This brings me to authors.

Parenting Your Book

I count myself lucky to have spent the entirety of my professional career working with a remarkable set of individuals called authors. These are power-people who are so deeply passionate about a particular story, subject, idea, or discipline that the gravity of their fascination compels words from their brains through their fingertips and onto the page, by the tens of thousands.

I can sense their excitement and confidence in their subject and their passion for sharing their wisdom, counsel, and experience. I know that it drives them to do great things and to touch others. It's a market I'm extremely fortunate to serve.

As of this writing, I'm nearly two decades into my career as a book designer. It'd be impossible to count how many publishing projects I've contributed to on some level. Conservatively, I'd put it around a thousand. I've worked with doctors, lawyers, professors, educators, pilots, athletes, therapists, chefs, executives, coaches, memoirists, nonprofit operators, and thought leaders of all kinds.

Until now, my credit has always been some form of "designer." Today, I present myself to you as an author. And now that I have gone through the rigors of bookwriting, I cannot ignore the parallels between authordom and parenthood, specifically with regard to why they are both so damned *hard*.

Kidless George felt the same way about parenting that Bookless George felt about authoring. In fact, I had logged considerably more hours observing authors than parents and *still* didn't fully grasp the bigger picture. I certainly knew it was no easy task pushing an idea through to the printed page. But not having been on the other side of the publishing equation, I didn't fully understand my assumptions.

Now, I do.

I understand that "hard" is not necessarily a matter of checking your grammar or meeting a deadline under pressure. As with parenting, the "hard" moments are the ones you don't see, which comprise the great Author Onion.

> "Hard" is staring at a blinking cursor, wondering why I can't conjure the next sentence. *I know what I'm trying to get across—why won't my brain tell my fingers how to write it?*

> "Hard" is poring over my editor's comments, repeatedly feeling the sting of (valid) criticism, and realizing that a few hundred words that I was once extremely proud of actually make no sense.

> "Hard" is lying awake at 2 a.m., wondering if my hours of effort will all be for naught. "Did I completely miss the mark? Will anyone read this? Was it all a waste of time?"

That last example brings me to my *why*.

Every creator—author, musician, designer, the list goes on—grapples with imposter syndrome and self-doubt. They invest hours, days, months, maybe even years into a project, hoping dearly that it might improve their standing, invite new opportunities, or merely provide self-worth.

But authors who are developing a book without a publisher's resources—as so many of us are (and should) in this day and age—fully assume the risk. There is pressure to ensure every phase is well executed, lest we take an inferior product to market.

Since launching my book design practice in 2019, I have learned that it is incumbent upon me to perform in a capacity greater than "designer." There is an element of project management and consultation that authors desire from their book designer, whether or not they realize it at the onset of the project. While most authors instinctively recognize the value of a great editor, many engage with me thinking all they need is a *product*. Our collaboration is often well underway before they recognize what they *really* want in a book designer: someone who will listen, communicate, coach, encourage, empathize, and embrace their goals.

While I'm grateful that many authors place their faith in my process without fully comprehending how important these qualities are, it revealed something to me about the market: *today's independent author needs help understanding the real value of a book designer.*

> Today's independent author needs help understanding the real value of a book designer.

That is the aim of this book. I want more authors to confidently say, "That was worth it" at the end of their book design experience. And I believe the chances of this are much higher if they develop an understanding of the anatomy of a great book design collaboration *before* they select a resource. As with any investment—car buying, stocks, real estate—the informed consumer is equipped to make better decisions. I want this book to provide you with that leverage.

During my first seventeen years of serving the independent author community, I could not view the process through the author's eyes. Writing this book has imbued me with a fresh perspective. That alone has more than validated the hours and the expense.

Just as I hope you, the soon-to-be author, will be able to better navigate this exciting and transformative process of book design after reading this book, I can now better empathize with *your* experience after writing it.

Authoring, much like parenting, is "hard but worth it." I hope this book makes it a bit easier—and a bit more worth it.

Yours in design,
George B. Stevens

INTRODUCTION

BOOK DESIGN MATTERS

It was in George Eliot's 1860 novel *The Mill on the Floss* where the infamous platitude made one of its earliest recorded debuts.[2] "One mustn't judge [a book] by th' outside," was the form it took, but it's a modernized version of this idiom that we've all heard since grade school:

> *"Never judge a book by its cover."*

Regardless of how readily you accept this advice, there is a specific context in which it can be virtually impossible to apply.

And that, of course, is an *actual* book and its cover.[3]

Ye Will Be Judged!

A book's design is directly linked to its value. This is especially true of nonfiction authors who are seeking to position themselves as a vital market resource. Having operated in the self-publishing

2 "Can't Judge a Book by Its Cover." *The Idioms.* February 13, 2016. https://www. theidioms.com/cant-judge-a-book-by-its-cover/

3 In the context of the phrase, "cover" should be taken to mean all elements of the book design: jacket, interior formatting, etc.

space for nearly two decades, I've encountered countless books that had their messages diluted by a bargain-bin cover and a clunky interior layout.

This is a real tragedy. You, a current and/or future author, are keenly aware of the unbelievable amount of effort it takes to write a manuscript. It asks so much of you: time, fortitude, stamina, money. Not to mention the life's worth of experiences that informed your writing.

You are also aware of the immense value that being a published author creates. I have worked on books for business professionals to whom a single new client might mean *seven figures* of added revenue. The return on their investment in publishing services stands to be astronomical.

Still, some authors underrate the importance of book design. Worse yet, some view it as a perfunctory step that can be accomplished via the path of least resistance. I believe there are two primary factors that feed this mindset:

1. Having endured an exhausting writing process, the author is out of gas, budgetarily tapped, "over it."

2. The author doesn't know enough about the resources available to them, so they default to the first Google result or the lowest bidder.

> **Some authors view book design as a perfunctory step that can be accomplished via the path of least resistance.**

This book will address both of these factors, but let's spend some time discussing the latter, because I think it's the more dangerous of the two. It's also the more understandable factor.

After all, commissioning a book designer is not an everyday task. It's a service no one thinks about until the moment they need it. As such, defaulting to the first Google result is a reasonable instinct.

But is it the right one?

Let it be known that big-box purveyors of "fast and cheap" services put a *lot* of effort into appearing on the first page of search results. Once they've won the SEO battle, they'll lure plenty of none-the-wiser authors into taking what could prove to be a damaging shortcut.

I'll dig into the different book design resources in chapter 3, but a good rule of thumb is to beware of any design service that places the burden of selection on the author; in other words, those that ask you to choose your cover from a slate of "options." This is not how design works! Remember, in an array of bad options, the best one is still a bad option. Even worse, it will look good by comparison.

The design process is *not* about selecting an "option." It's the result of a collaborative and iterative process, one that involves two contributing parties: the skilled consultant (a.k.a. the designer) and the subject matter expert (a.k.a. the client). I'm writing this book to arm you, the venerable author, with an understanding of what *your* role is in that process. If you approach it thoughtfully and meaningfully, your book will be stronger for it. Your manuscript will sing because it's well packaged and smartly typeset. Your cover will stand out from the thousands of titles released every day by authors who *didn't* embrace process-driven design.

The first step is to dismiss the notion that only Very Important Authors™ authors can have nice-looking books.

Shaking the Stigma of "Self-Published"

I hear it all the time:

"Just don't make my book look self-published."

It is the most common artistic direction I receive from authors. And it's never phrased, "Don't make it look cheap and tacky," or "It needs to look like it matters."

It's always, "Don't make it look self-published."[4]

I hear this from the same authors who are quick to champion self-publishing as their most strategically and financially beneficial publishing approach. And they're not wrong: when you consider all the factors in play, independently publishing is the smartest approach for most authors. It's no longer the consolation prize for those who fail to garner the attention of a major publisher. Self-publishing platforms allow authors to produce books that are available worldwide, with no minimum print cost and without compromising intellectual property. I believe, unhyperbolically, that self-publishing is one of the wonders of the modern world.

"But remember . . . it can't *look* self-published."

We can draw an important conclusion from this: there is a disconnect between the perceived value of self-publishing and that of the graphic design resources that support it. Why?

---

4 Congratulations, you found the title of the book!

> There is a disconnect between the perceived value of self-publishing and that of the graphic design resources that support it.

In the early days of self-publishing, books were *expected* to look DIY and amateurish due to constraints in production. Simply put, for most individuals, it cost too much to produce a nice-looking book. Financial backing from a publisher was a must—without it, you did the best you could at a local print shop (think copy paper and plastic binding combs.)

Along came the digital press, which gave authors the ability to print actual books at low cost and without minimum quantities. Self-publishing became more viable, and it was not long before a correlating service ecosystem evolved.

Today, self-publishing authors have access to the same caliber of editorial, design, and marketing talent as traditionally published authors. This can be traced to two major factors:

1. The rise of on-demand printing and DIY publishing and distribution platforms

2. The explosion of the gig economy, thanks in part to remote viability

In short, it's now easier than ever to print and distribute books *and* to find the support you need to get your book looking and reading like a high-end publication. Hordes of talented editors, publishing coordinators, book designers, marketers, and publicists with considerable industry experience have set out to serve the self-publishing community. The gap between resources available to "the big boys" and the DIY crowd has all but vanished.[5]

However, the scourge of shoddy self-publishing projects persists. Despite the strides the industry has made and the vast pool of talent that supports it, many authors still end up with a book that reads and looks, shall we say, *uncompetitive.*

Of course, this is *good* news for those who recognize the value of mindfully approaching the book design process. *Your* book will stand out from the scads of low-rent releases. In an era when credibility is king, a book that positions you as a less-than-essential resource could be your checkmate.

> **In an era when credibility is king, a book that positions you as a less-than-essential resource could be your checkmate.**

Imagine: You're being considered for a keynote speech at a Fortune 500 company's annual corporate retreat. The payday is eye-popping for an hour-long speech and a breakout session. Good thing you recently published a book to bolster your credibility. You tuck it into your press kit and mail it to the event planner.

---

5 The notable exception here is the printed product. A major crux of what makes self-publishing viable is the cost efficiency of digitally printed books. And while digital printing technologies produce impressive physical books and will continue to evolve, the fact is that traditional (a.k.a. "offset") printing still yields the highest quality product. But given the investment required to make traditional printing viable from a unit cost perspective—five-figure investments are not uncommon for offset print runs—the quality gap isn't close to worth it for most self-publishing authors.

Now, if your cover was rush designed for pennies on the dollar[6] and looks like it belongs on a thrift store shelf, what will it signal to the planner? My guess would be something along the lines of, "Not the caliber of speaker we're looking for."

They open another candidate's press kit and find a book that is smartly designed, looking every bit the part of a *New York Times* bestseller.

If you were that event planner, would this make for a difficult decision?

My hope is that reading this book will help you become the latter candidate in that scenario. I want to fortify your understanding of the publishing design process so that you can make informed decisions every step of the way, from hiring the right resource to positively impacting the collaboration. This also includes budgeting. If you can get a sense of what's important to you in a design partner, you will have a better idea of how much you're willing to invest.

Cracking the Book

I want to arm you with tools and knowledge that enable you to approach publishing design the right way. I want to empower you with an understanding of *your* role in the process. I want you to have the confidence to approach this critical stage of the publishing process in a way that yields excellent results.

Since I started designing books in 2007, I've partnered with hundreds and hundreds of individuals who had something to say.

---

6 While I believe there is a powerful correlation between investment and quality, I will note throughout this book that money is *not* necessarily the magic bullet. Ultimately, every designer should be able to explain their rates. Read on for more on how to recognize value in your potential book design resources.

These people scatter the planet: I've worked with authors from every continent[7] and most US states. Their publishing ambitions are similarly widespread. I've designed books that landed on the *New York Times* bestseller list, but I've also designed books that exist for personal fulfillment, distributed only to a small number of friends and family.

This is the beauty of modern self-publishing. It supports a broad spectrum of publishing ambitions, which is important because *every* book—including yours and mine—is published with a unique set of goals in mind. And these goals are more likely to be reached if that book is produced with skill, intention, and a full embrace of purpose by the person responsible for designing it.

This book is broken into two parts:

> **Part 1** focuses on finding a designer who is right for you. Make no mistake: *who you hire* is the single most critical factor in ensuring excellent results. Every outcome will trickle down from that single decision. The first part of this book will help you understand value in a design relationship, the various resources at your disposal, and how you can best evaluate these providers vis-a-vis your own project.

> **Part 2** moves into the design process itself. What so many authors fail to recognize is their own importance in the creative process. Just because you're depending on specialized talent does not mean you aren't bringing an immense measure of value to the equation. We'll

---

7 Okay, I admit it: not Antarctica. If any Antarctica-based researchers are reading this book, please reach out.

discuss each phase of the book build and how you can impact the active process and drive excellent results.

This book will help you find your dream designer. It'll help your book look as strong as any major release and like one that you can share with pride and confidence. It will help you avoid the trappings of low-rent design that so many self-publishing authors fall into.

Let's dig in, and remember: Self-publishing is a beautiful thing. *Looking* self-published is not.

```
┌─────────────────────────────────┐
│  ┌───────────────────────────┐  │
│  │       P A R T   1         │  │
│  └───────────────────────────┘  │
│  ┌───────────────────────────┐  │
│  │         FINDING           │  │
│  │          YOUR             │  │
│  │        DESIGNER           │  │
│  └───────────────────────────┘  │
└─────────────────────────────────┘
```

Welcome to the part of this book that matters most.

Yes, I am taking the self-sabotaging tack of telling you at the outset that one half of this book is more important than the other. And it's not because the second half—which focuses on the author's role in an active design collaboration—is devoid of valuable information. However, its value is corrupted if the first half of the book isn't fully embraced.

It's a point I'll hammer repeatedly throughout this book: *who you hire* is the most critical decision you'll make in the entire design process. No matter how prepared you are for the process, tapping the right design resource will be the biggest difference-maker when the rubber hits the road. On the other hand, the *wrong* designer could make for an uncomfortable and dysfunctional experience.

The other reason I'm putting an emphasis on making the right hire is because I believe it is the most overlooked inflection point in the self-publishing experience. When thinking about the book design, most authors put the cart before the horse. They contemplate the cover and maybe think through some layout elements. In short, they worry how the book design will come together, not who will manage the process. It's an understandable instinct, but you've got to keep your priorities straight. Remember: the "*how*" might go terribly wrong without the right "*who*" on your team.

If all this has you asking, "*What?*" … read on!

THE THREE TRUTHS OF BOOK DESIGN

*Laying the Foundation
for Your Search*

STOP EVERYTHING!

Before we continue, my crack team of publishing advisors has insisted that I explain why this book includes a chapter zero.

Two reasons: *everyone* I asked to review this book had a reaction to seeing that "Chapter 0" heading. We creative types call that a win.

Granted, most of the comments were calling it into question, which leads me to the second reason.

There is a specific definition of "zero" that applies here: "origin." As in, patient zero. Ground zero. Zero hour. Mathematically speaking, "one" suggests the fulfillment of a single unit—*zero* is where it all begins. As such, Chapter Zero outlines a trio of simple concepts that I believe are critical to fully absorbing the value of this book.

Embrace these three truths, and you'll maximize your ability to appreciate the ideas presented throughout this book.

Now, on to the chapter . . . chapter zero, that is.

Self-publishing a book is a lot like general-contracting the construction of a new home. You have full control over the outcome and quality of your final product but are responsible for curating all phases of the project. In the case of your book, this would include editorial, admin/distribution, marketing, and—you guessed it—design.

If you want to maximize the benefits of self-publishing, it's important to understand the value of the professionals you're hiring. Spend a bit of time learning about the various stakeholders in your publishing journey and you'll set yourself apart from those who blow through the process cheaply and cantankerously. *Those* individuals will end up with a book that could be described similarly. Meanwhile, you'll enter the market with a book that looks like it matters. This will encourage your market to recognize you as a subject matter expert.

Authors are often anxious about how their manuscript will transition from an unadorned document into a beautifully jacketed and typeset book.

When contemplating their book's design, innumerable questions plague the aspiring author:

- ➡ What should be on the cover?
- ➡ What's the best color scheme for my market?
- ➡ What font family and size should be used for the book's text?
- ➡ Does the foreword come before the preface?[8]

This list could continue for pages because there are thousands of questions worth asking when it comes to book design.

---

8 Yes, per the *Chicago Manual of Style*.

The good news is that every last one of them rolls up into a single decision that, if approached thoughtfully, will set the table for success: **hiring the right book design resource.** Addressing *this* need should be priority number one, because a great book designer is equipped to guide you through the process with skill and confidence. This will result not only in a stunning book but also a rewarding collaboration that will usher you confidently into the marketplace.

But where to begin your search? Google will lay out a wide array of design resources available to self-publishing authors. From there, many opt for the quickest fix or the lowest bidder (which are often the same). You may recognize these culprits as "fast" and "cheap" in the *"Good, fast, cheap: pick two!"* paradigm. All too often, "good" finds itself on the outside looking in.

> **Many opt for the quickest fix or the lowest bidder (which are often the same). All to often, "good" is on the outside looking in.**

For the record, I don't blame the author. The vast, uneven landscape of design resources makes finding the *right* partner confusing and overwhelming. The temptation to follow what appears to be a path of least resistance is strong. But the reality is, authors who opt for "fast and cheap" resources are often left with iffy work, little support, and a sense of lingering uncertainty that makes pushing the "publish" button a paralyzing prospect.

How do I know this? I receive a steady flow of inquiries from authors who got burned by a quick-fix, low-budget resource. This includes authors who had previously reached out to me for an estimate but opted for a lower bidder. Unfortunately, they learned the hard way that underestimating the importance of the book design process can be a recipe for headache.

The worst part is that I often hear some version of, "I paid the cheap designer to go away, and now I'm ready to do it right." While I'm glad they saw the light, I wish they'd seen it *before* they made the investment in an inadequate resource. Now they're paying my rate *plus* the "thanks for your time" tax to get the cheap designer to disappear.

If I can steer one author away from such a fate, this book will have been worth it.

Before we launch into part 1 of this book, which will focus on hiring the right designer, a few general concepts about book design must be understood. This secret chapter will help organize your thinking so you can go forth into the designer search with confidence and clarity. In short, hiring the right resource begins with understanding a few basic concepts about book design and the people who do it.

> **Hiring the right resource begins with understanding a few basic concepts about book design and the people who do it.**

What follows are **three truths of book design that will help refine your search for the ideal design resource**.

Truth #1: Design Is a Process, Not a Product

This is a fundamental principle that must be understood before you begin your search. When you agree to the rate of a book designer, you are not "buying" the book cover. You are investing in a collaboration. This collaborative process results in the book cover.

This can be a revelation to those who are commissioning design for the first time. One might assume that, because the result of the collaboration is a product, you are simply "buying" the design. But more accurately, it's the designer's *process* that you are investing in.

As you're vetting designers, dig into their process and see how it conforms with the way you prefer to collaborate. For example, do you value autonomy in a designer—someone who can confidently make small decisions and only involve you at critical touchpoints?

Or would you prefer a designer who will check in with you on a daily basis and brief you on progress?

There's no one right answer, only what's right for *you*. Your ideal book designer should be fundamentally skilled but also able to complement your communication style and workflow preferences. This will create the optimal experience for you, which in turn will result in the best outcome.

➡ How Does This Factor into Budget?

"You get what you pay for" is a readily embraced concept of consumer economics. By reframing "what you pay for" as a *process* involving a skilled specialist—not a rectangular graphic—it could inform how you budget for your project.

Again, consider what *you* want out of the process. This will help you recognize value in your candidates.

BEFORE WE CONTINUE:
A Brief Word about Money and Budget Specifics

Throughout this book, I mainly write about cost in relative terms. There is a pricing example in chapter 3, but it is purposefully generic. This may annoy some readers who think I'm dancing around the money talk by avoiding real figures.

As I will assert repeatedly, there is no standard pricing template for book design, particularly when an interior layout process is involved.

There are a zillion factors that feed into any given project estimate, many of which I will discuss throughout this book. They include the individual service provider, the nature of the work, timing goals, and even the economic climate. And as with just about anything—houses, cars, eggs—costs change over time.

As such, I am hesitant to risk creating a subconscious expectation within my individual readers by dropping dollar amounts.

Instead, this book will give you the tools to understand relative value in book design, and from there you can get real estimates from real designers and weigh that information against your newfound knowledge.

With that said, your book will cost one million dollars to design. Call your financial planner now.[9]

---

9 Only kidding. Unless you weren't bothered by that number, in which case, I am currently available for new commissions and would love to discuss your project.

Truth #2: Book Design Is a Specialty

Not all doctors are pediatricians.

Not all musicians are jazz pianists.

Not all graphic designers are book designers.

Each of these is an example of a specialist within a broader field. Book designers have a refined understanding of the technical components of book layout and composition. They follow trends, understand how to interact with book printers, and anticipate obstacles that may arise throughout a design process.

> **Not all doctors are pediatricians.**
> **Not all musicians are jazz pianists.**
> **Not all graphic designers are book designers.**

Another benefit of hiring a specialist is that they're likely connected to a stable of corollary resources. Need a proofreader? An illustrator? A PR expert? Maybe someone to coordinate the publishing and distribution of your book? Chances are, a tenured book designer knows someone and can provide a quality referral. The value of a great book designer extends well beyond their core abilities. (See the chart on page 79 for a deeper dive into this concept.)

Of course, there *are* graphic design generalists who might raise their hand for a book design project, but their business model often relies on volume. The depth of service you receive may be less than someone who spends all day, every day designing books.

To again draw a comparison to doctors: Think of these "jack-of-all trades" designers as general practitioners. If the ailment you're experiencing is common and/or quickly resolved, it's likely that they'll be an adequate resource. However, if your issue is nuanced and requires time-intensive care, you'll probably be referred to a specialist.

There are two reasons for this: First, a GP's expertise may stop short of allowing them to confidently diagnose and treat your issue. Second, a GP may not have the bandwidth to deep dive into your issue, so they'd just as soon refer you to someone who does.

It's the same concept with book design (or branding design, UI/UX, or any specialty). I often get referrals from designers who won't touch books, and I'm just as happy to get the project as they are to pass it along. Likewise, I usually refer nonpublishing requests to other specialists. This keeps my focus on books and points the prospect to a better resource.

Of course, there is nothing wrong with being a general medical practitioner or graphic designer. But if *your* needs are specific, generalists may not be a fit.

➡ How Does This Factor into Budget?

As is the case in any industry, specialists are going to command a higher rate. But the understanding is that you'll receive commensurate *value*, both during the process and beyond it. Remember, your book is not an ephemeral asset with a short lifespan, like social media posts or event flyers. **If you intend to leverage it as a prestige marketing tool that can serve as a platform for years to come, investing in a book design specialist could pay for itself many times over.**

Truth #3: Beware of Options

We've established that design is a process, not a product. But many prominent design resources run on a business model that ditches process for *options*.

The psychological trick these resources play is to dazzle the client with *quantity*. It's a numbers game: if they show you enough choices, at least one of them will look appealing by comparison.

But as the saying goes, "The best of a set of bad options is still a bad option."

My rule of thumb: **beware of any resource, be it an individual or a business, that places the burden on you to decide what great design is by asking you to choose from options.**

My stance is that "options" is a bad word in design. If you hear it, run for the hills. Okay, I'm being intentionally pedantic here. If you've worked with a designer who uses the word "options," it doesn't mean they are scamming you. But you *should* expect your designer to engage in an iterative process that doesn't put unreasonable restrictions on the development of your book's design. The winning solution is one at which you should confidently and mutually arrive. You shouldn't feel pressured to *settle*.

Strive to hire a designer who will spend time learning about you, your message, your voice, and your market *before* initiating the design phase. Then they should show you *concepts*, with the understanding that there will be the opportunity for iteration and evolution.

➡ How Does This Factor into Budget?

It may seem paradoxical, but I believe the more you invest, the fewer designs you'll stand to see. This is a feature, not a bug. In my experience, authors aren't interested in parsing through an array of half-cooked concepts with the hope they'll see something worth exploring. Most prefer a small selection of ideas that are based on a meaningful discussion and agreed-upon direction.

You must remember that different designers embrace different approaches. Some may prefer to design a single fully realized cover and iterate from there. Others may show you four or five or ten solid proofs of concept. There's no wrong answer, but as I've emphasized, it behooves you to dig into each candidate's process *before* you hire them so that you can evaluate your comfort level with these factors. This way, you'll be sure you're getting more than just "options."

DESIGNECDOTE[10]
Quantity over Quality

I was once hired by an author who was freshly disengaged from a different book designer. She told me her previous designer sent her upward of *fifty* cover drafts. This seemed unbelievable. But when she shared them with me, I realized the designer had simply swapped out the title matter and imagery of a bunch of cheesy templates to make them appear vaguely customized for the author's project. Of course, there was little to no depth of quality. Dismayed, the author decided to move on.

By contrast, she and I explored three initial concepts, iterated on one of them, and within a few weeks had arrived at her winning solution. She was extremely pleased with her cover and the experience on the whole.

---

10 Throughout this book, you'll encounter "Designecdotes" (design + anecdote). These entries are derived from my two decades of experience as a client-facing book designer and will help practically illustrate the concepts being discussed.

Taking It from Here

As you consider the best design resource for your book project, embrace these three concepts to weed out weak candidates.

When vetting resources, look for red flags, such as:

➡ unwillingness to be flexible from a process and communication standpoint

   Ex: "I only communicate through email."

➡ a lack of specialized knowledge

   Ex: "I've never designed a book, but don't worry, all design is the same."

➡ restrictive language

   Ex: "You get two options and one round of revisions."

Each of these factors speaks to a design resource that will not provide the depth of service that yields a great collaboration.

No matter how robust a search you're prepared to conduct, you must take your search further than a simple portfolio review. Work samples are important, but it's the baseline form of evaluation. If you like what you see in a designer's portfolio, you should then measure that resource against the Three Truths:

1. **Get a sense of how they conduct a design project. Have them walk you through their process.**

2. **Learn about their experience and philosophy when it comes to book design.**

3. **Be sure they allow for iteration and exploration of ideas as the design evolves.**

I'll close by acknowledging that most of my advice in this chapter points to not skimping on book design. "Of course a *book designer* would say that," you might be thinking.

Admittedly, one of my go-to lines is "cheap design gets you cheap design." But this chapter is not about encouraging you to spend more money. It's about helping you identify value.

I'll reiterate this point consistently: spending more money is not a magic bullet. Just because one design resource is charging ten times the rate of another does *not* automatically make them that much better.

No matter how much you're willing or able to invest in the process, it's incumbent upon you to gain an understanding of a designer's value *before* agreeing to work with them. Just as you shouldn't default to the quick fix or cheapest option, don't assume that a designer who charges prestige rates is automatically the best choice. By conducting your search for a book designer with these Three Truths in mind, you'll home in on a resource that provides the balance of cost and value that is unique to your project.

DESIGN DEBRIEF
CHAPTER ZERO: THE THREE TRUTHS OF BOOK DESIGN

Design Is a Process, Not a Product

You're investing in a collaborative experience, not just paying for a finished cover. A great designer brings guidance, iteration, and expertise throughout the journey.

Book Design Is a Specialty

Not all designers are created equal. Just like you wouldn't see a general practitioner for heart surgery, you shouldn't hire a generalist for a book design project.

Beware of "Options"

Avoid resources that hand you a menu of choices. True design is iterative and custom-built from your voice and message. It is not about settling on a "best fit" solution.

THE CRITICAL FIRST STEP

Keeping the Dream Alive

Author's Note: Don't have time for this chapter? Just read the final word of the third paragraph and move along. However, I'd encourage you to revisit this chapter if you're stalled, stuck, sapped, or otherwise need to remind yourself why you're writing this book.

"T-H-E E-N-D"

Six final keystrokes that signify something magical.

Believe it: you've completed your manuscript. And there's a critical step you *must* take before you do anything else: *Celebrate*.

Pop that champagne. High five your dog. Breakdance in your living room, if that's your thing. However you choose to do it, *celebrate*. You've done something to which many aspire, yet few will ever accomplish.

Sadly, too many authors forget to bask in their moment of glory. Instead, they hand their manuscript off with a shrug and a sigh. This is the result of having slogged through an exhaustive period of writing and editing. "I'm over it," is something I hear often from in-process authors. "Take this thing away from me. I just want to be done."

The Fantasy

Perhaps you envisioned things playing out differently.

Your writing process was *supposed* to be a quaint, romantic affair befitting a Hallmark movie. You would sequester in a snowbound mountain cabin. The fireplace would hiss and crackle as you clack away on a rustic typewriter, pausing for the occasional sip of chamomile or contemplative chin scratch. After a few dreamy weeks of unyielding output, the moment arrives: cut to an extreme closeup of typebars slapping the long-awaited letter string onto your final page: T-H-E E-N-D.

The Reality

Record scratch: your actual writing experience wasn't quite so charming.

The process was as grueling as a marathon and as taxing as— well, doing your taxes. You bashed it out a few paragraphs at a time, usually early in the morning or late at night. If you were able to block off half an hour during your workday for a dedicated writing session, you'd consider yourself lucky. You'd go weeks without touching it, then delete full pages or chapters that didn't sound as good when you revisited them. Finally, over the course of months or years, you arrived at something resembling a manuscript.

At least the last part is the same: T-H-E E-N...

Hold the phone! You're advised to invest in editorial services, some of which you didn't even know existed. *A "line edit"? What the hell is that?* You're assured it's essential and worth every dollar. And so are the other three editorial passes.[11] By now, you've been subjected to so many edits that you can hardly remember writing the words in the first place.

I never want to read this thing again, you think, as you're asked to review yet another slate of needling editorial commentary.

Finally, you receive an email from your copy editor. "The edit is complete! Final manuscript attached. (Invoice also attached.)" And, indeed, there at the bottom of the email is the ultimate talisman: the legendary *completed manuscript.*

By now, you've invested countless hours and a small fortune into this project. *And it all led to this moment.* You should be geysering dopamine, basking in a rich aura of accomplishment!

Instead, you feel nothing. You're numb. You're over it. The thrill is gone.

You are presently suffering from an acute case of Self-Publishing Author's Disenchantment Syndrome. Side effects of SPADS include mental fatigue, self-doubt, and selective amnesia (as in, "I don't remember why I thought this was a good idea").

No one can blame you for feeling this way. You've been through a gauntlet. But I encourage you not to lose sight of your achievement. Remember: you now share a commonality with the names Twain, Bronte, Steinbeck, and Morrison. It's important to take a moment to revel in what you've accomplished. Do not downplay it. Say it with me: *you wrote a book.*

---

11 For the record, I'm not making light of the valuable services my editorial colleagues provide. I believe fortifying your manuscript through these editorial stages *is* worth the investment. But it adds up!

So I'll say it again: go celebrate! After all, you've reached the top of the mountain.

Wait a second.

The top? Aren't you *over* the mountain? Back at sea level, primed to bask in the spoils of authordom?

Not quite. Let's talk about the mountain.

DESIGN DEBRIEF!
CHAPTER 1: THE CRITICAL FIRST STEP

Celebrate!

Finishing your manuscript is a rare and impressive feat. Don't let burnout rob you of the pride in your accomplishment.

Reality Bites

The dream of a therapeutic writing process clashes with the true grind of writing amidst life's chaos.

Self-Publishing Disenchantment

It's common to feel numb and sapped of motivation after finishing your manuscript. This is a symptom, not a failure.

Reignite Your Why

Reflect on the deeper reasons you started writing. It helps you push forward into the next phase with purpose.

DIY(NBY)

Do It Yourself (Not By Yourself)

If you have just finished the first chapter of this book, I'm going to assume your heart is thumping after a rousing victory lap or two around your front yard. I trust that you sprinted down your street shouting, "I wrote a book!" to each person, car, cat, and birdfeeder you passed. And I hope you're feeling reinvigorated for this final push toward publication: the design process that will transform your brilliant manuscript from a workmanlike Word document into a dazzlingly jacketed and formatted book.

There's no arguing that you've accomplished something rare and impressive, but there is still important work to do. The chapter you're about to read will provide some perspective on what's left of your journey and help you understand the important role a book designer plays in your publishing team.

The Peak Is Only Halfway

If you read business nonfiction with any regularity, you've no doubt encountered analogies that employ mountain climbing as a metaphor for tackling goals. And in these examples, the ultimate achievement is typically represented by reaching the peak.

This is fair play when it comes to completing your manuscript. But I believe this metaphor breaks down when you consider the publishing project at large.

Yes, finishing your manuscript is a major accomplishment. You've achieved something few ever will. As a writer, you've planted your flag on a hallowed peak. **One problem: your potential readers are not with you on the peak.** They're back down at ground level, going about their business. And if they're going to find out what you have to say, you'd better bring your message down that mountain. (Moses had to do it, and so do you.)

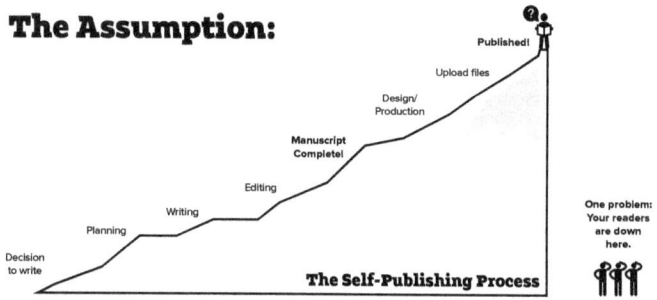

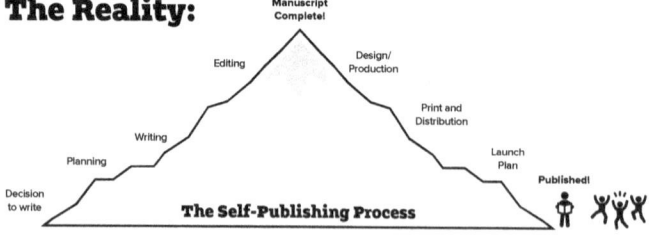

Anyone who's gone hiking—whether it was a multiday back-packing excursion or a casual day hike—understands that a payoff view requires two distinct efforts: getting there and getting back. The farther out you have to hike, the better the view, but also the farther the hike back down to your point of origin.

Publishing your book is no casual day hike. Reaching your mountaintop—that is, putting a bow on your manuscript—is one of the toughest climbs you'll ever make. But once you've ascended (and, don't forget, *celebrated*), it's every bit as critical that you approach your hike down to the marketplace in a thoughtful and strategic manner.

Gee, wouldn't it be quicker and easier to free-roll down the mountainside? Technically, yes, if you're okay with fractures, gashes, and concussions. Remember: If you fall down a mountain, no one celebrates the fact that you climbed it. They'll only remember the fall.

When you get down the mountain, how do you want *your* audience to react? Awestruck by your accomplishment or repelled by your condition?

> **How do you want your audience to react?**
> **Awestruck by your accomplishment or**
> **repelled by your condition?**

Just as the most daring mountaineers enlist guides to avoid unwanted missteps, every successful self-published author is the benefactor of professional guidance. And that shouldn't be a revelation. Reliable support when taking on something audacious and complex is a no-brainer, whether that "something" is scaling Mt. Everest or publishing your own book.

Your editor(s) helped you reach the peak, but a unique set of circumstances and challenges await on the way down. Getting your book designed is *not* a retread of the writing process. It's a separate hike altogether. It stands to reason that you need distinct, specialized help. You want someone who is familiar with the trail, who knows where the snags and pitfalls lurk, and who will make sure you emerge from the trail looking like someone with an important story to tell.

Let's get you down the mountain.

DESIGN DEBRIEF!
CHAPTER 2: DIY(NBY)

The Journey Isn't Over

Completing your manuscript is only halfway to the summit. You now must carry your message back "down the mountain" to your readers.

Support Is Essential

Successful authors don't go it alone. Just like mountaineers rely on guides, authors need professional help.

DIY vs. NBY

"Do it yourself" doesn't mean do it alone. Seek pros who can elevate your work, not just do tasks.

Bad Design Undercuts Good Work

A poorly designed book masks your brilliance. You've done the hard part—don't tumble down the final stretch.

Professional Design = Reader Respect

Design isn't decoration. It's the delivery mechanism for your message. Respect the journey by finishing strong.

THE HUNT FOR A BOOK DESIGNER

Three Critical Questions to Define Your Search

Whether you're at the top of the mountain or are merely mapping out your trek from square one, the design phase is looming. And as an independent author, *you* are tasked with finding the book design resource that's right for you.

Commissioning book design is something for which you probably have no basis. It simply isn't a need that most of us encounter with regularity. Perhaps you once hired a graphic designer to create your company's logo or frame out your business cards. Maybe your company has a staff designer.

Remember the second truth of book design: book design is a specialty. Your branding designer *probably* isn't a book designer. If you want to maximize your book's potential, your focus should be on hiring a *specialist*.

Let's find one.

Defining Your Search

This chapter will help you answer three simple questions that provide structure to your search:

1. **What am I investing in?**

2. **How much should I budget?**

3. **Where should I look?**

Why are these questions important? As the self-publishing industry has flourished, so has the resource network that supports it. The rise of the gig economy has yielded hordes of freelance editors and designers the world over looking for book projects. Crowdsourcing platforms have emerged, nurturing communities that connect authors and freelance publishing professionals. There are also vanity publishing houses and creative agencies that offer a more traditional, turnkey experience to authors with the resources to invest in it.

No matter how you go about it, choosing your book design resource is a major inflection point in the publishing process. In fact, I dedicated the entirety of the first half of this book to the subject, because I believe it's that important.

What follows are a few questions you should have an answer to *before* beginning your search.

1. What Am I Investing In?

Yes, *investing*. You must view book design as an investment, not a consumption good or lifestyle expense. This is especially true if you intend to leverage your book as a lead generator or personal brand. You are investing in something that will create immense value and, ideally, pay for itself many times over.

And of course, you must understand what you're spending money on *before* you determine a sensible amount to invest.

We all accept that a higher sticker price generally correlates with the expectation of higher value. For example, a fifty-thousand-dollar vehicle *should* have more going for it than a ten-thousand-dollar vehicle. The price jump may be accounted for by gadgetry, reliability, safety and comfort features, gas mileage, product support, and other practical considerations.

So how does this translate to book design?

In order to help you understand the value of book design, we must revisit the first principle discussed in chapter zero: when you pay a designer's rate, you're not *buying* the book cover. This would suggest that design is a product, which it is not. Remember: design is a *service* that *results* in a product. You are investing in that service.

As with any service, its quality is informed by a designer's strengths in a variety of areas, including:

- ➡ technical ability
- ➡ efficiency
- ➡ industry experience
- ➡ communication skills
- ➡ project management
- ➡ collaborative spirit

Certain strengths may be more important to you than others. For example, you may be willing to work with a book designer who has limited experience if you determine they're an efficient worker and you click with them on a personal level (file under "collaborative spirit").

With any designer you consider, you've got to weigh their strengths against their rate. I'll say it again: "You get what you pay for" is as true with book design as it is with any service field. Just as you'd expect a Ritz-Carlton to provide a better lodging experience than a Motel 6, expect designers whose rates are higher to provide more value in their collaborations.

> **"You get what you pay for"**
> **is as true with book design**
> **as it is with any service field.**

The Ritz famously provides a custom experience that caters to your needs and personality. Similarly, a high-value designer will seek to understand your drivers, your goals, your market, your work style—in other words, *you*. They'll fuse that understanding with their practical expertise to curate an enjoyable process and ultimately generate the design that lives in your mind's eye.

Furthermore, they'll carry out the project with a spirit of service and support. A great designer understands that developing a collaborative relationship takes time. A cut-rate designer might downplay the need for communication and limit your opportunity for iteration. The omission of these factors lessens the likelihood of a great experience *or* an outstanding design.

I don't belabor this point strictly to convince you to drop big bucks on design work. Rather, my goal is to underscore the realities of a design relationship—realities many budget resources hope to obscure. If you encounter a design resource—be it an individual designer or a branded service—that touts low prices and speed of service, just remember that something else has to give. Deals that sound too good to be true often are.

2. How Much Should I Budget?

Let's move on to the sexiest question of the three: What amount should you budget for book design?

There are a few basic concepts to embrace when budgeting for book design:

→ **Every book project is unique.** Your estimate should be specific to your project. One-size-fits-all pricing can be a dangerous prospect for both you and your designer.

→ **"Good, fast, cheap: pick two."** You've heard it before, but it's as true in book design as anything. On that note, I'll continue to drive this next point home . . .

→ **Avoid "fast and cheap," and beware of "good and cheap."** Regardless of the other factors, remember my mantra: *cheap book design gets you cheap book design.* But worry not, because . . .

→ **A well-designed book can pay for itself.** Yes, I'm not-so-subtly suggesting that you shouldn't skimp on book design. I firmly believe that a beautifully designed book will not only position you as a market-worthy resource but also imbue you with an invaluable confidence that will help you remain energized throughout the book's monetization lifecycle. Both these factors translate to more and better opportunities. Perhaps a more concise and resonant way to frame this: *low-rent design risks positioning you as a low-rent resource.*

Disclaimer: *The first bullet is an objective truth. The next three are personal beliefs I've developed through nearly two decades of book design experience.*

A Pricing Example

As I just detailed, all projects are unique, and your book's design warrants a unique estimate. But in the interest of providing a measuring stick, let's look at a sample project that edges toward "typical." Of course, we'll be dealing in generalities, but the goal is to give you a sense of why certain practitioners charge what they do.

Sample Project

60,000-word manuscript for business/nonfiction book. Author is seeking comprehensive design collaboration.

➡ **Full jacket design:** Front cover, spine, back cover. This could include two to four unique cover design concepts and a reasonable period of iteration and revision.

➡ **Full layout design:** Sixty thousand words. Ten chapters. Moderate amount of formatting.

➡ **Ten simple graphics:** Charts or graphs within the manuscript that will visually conform with the prevailing style established by the cover design.

➡ **File preparation:** Paperback and digital formats.

➡ **Timeline:** Sixty business day production window.

This a fairly down-the-middle project by my standards. It represents a standard set of parameters for the sorts of business/nonfiction manuscripts I commonly see.

So, How Much?

Each estimate you receive for a given project will be different. This must be understood. This is where it gets tricky.

Let's first discuss the outliers. You might find book design resources that will quote you several hundred dollars (US) to tackle this job. I would be *deeply* suspicious of such a rate. It is simply not commensurate with inputs required to manage and execute this project to a degree that will yield outstanding results.

What about the other side of the bell curve? I'm slower to question prestige-level resources. If the world's greatest living painter charges a million bucks for a portrait, who's to say they aren't worth it? Still, extreme high-side outliers raise red flags of their own. Do they actually want the job? Are they playing a numbers game ("If I land one free-wheeling investor at this exorbitant rate, it'll make up for all the folks who laughed in my face!")?

Now let's discuss the Realm of the Reasonable. I am of the opinion that our Sample Project warrants a design investment in the lower thousands (US). A more experienced designer might edge beyond that.

If spending thousands on book design sounds unreasonable to you, consider the hourly breakdown. For a specialist who charges $50 an hour, a $3,000[12] job is akin to sixty hours. A week and a half of consistent work, spread out over a two-month timeline. Having executed more than a thousand book design processes, I can attest to this input being healthy and realistic for a standard business reader.[13]

Book design is a complex, time-consuming, and detail-laden undertaking. Specialists know it takes considerable time and focus to arrive at creative solutions, carry out the process in an expert manner, and fully support the author along the way. Do not be convinced otherwise by resources looking to lure you into "fast and cheap" solutions.

---

12 A reminder that I am not saying *your* book design process will cost $3,000. This is a purposefully generic example.

13 Once again, your book may take more time. Or less. Don't get hung up on the sixty hours thing—it's just an example!

For the designer charging $500, we're talking less than $10 per hour. How motivated do you think that individual will be to ensure high-quality work, service, and support? Or to spend a little extra time aligning elements within your cover art? Or to quickly answer your phone calls and emails?

Remember the second truth of book design: book design is a specialty. If someone *isn't* charging specialist rates, you shouldn't expect specialty work.[14] Over the course of a book design project, there are hundreds of opportunities to settle for "good enough." Your designer should be financially motivated to avoid shortcuts and give their all to the process.

DESIGNECDOTE
The Prodigal Author

Several years ago, I received outreach on a cover project via a crowdsourcing platform. The needs of the author were fairly standard: cover design process and file preparation for a paperback jacket. The author and I exchanged a few messages to define the scope of work, and then I sent over a proposal.

The author's response could best be described as a curt rejection. "Thank you for your proposal. Your price is much higher than other designers I've received proposals from, so I'll have to decline."

Frankly, this was not an uncommon response to project proposals via the crowdsourcing platform. I'd learned over time that its users were often working with lower

---

14 I acknowledge that there is an offshore workforce where this may constitute more than a living wage. It is certainly not impossible to find reliable design support in a far-away place, but you must consider factors like language barriers and time differences when it comes to project efficiency. For many of my authors, being able to quickly and clearly communicate with their publishing team is essential to the success of the project. If your budget dictates that exploring offshore support is necessary, it's all the more important that you carefully manage the project.

budgets. Compounding that, I have to inflate my rate to account for the 10 percent commission the platform claims. So rejection is the norm. I wished the author luck and moved on.

A month or so later, I received a message from this same author:

"Hello, George. I was wondering if you are still available for the project. In short, I hired one of the cheaper designers, and it has been a miserable experience. I paid out their rate so they'd disappear, and am now ready to invest in your services. Please let me know if you'd reconsider the project."

My heart broke for them.[15] And I couldn't help but feel a bit guilty for not warning them of this outcome, or at least making an effort to help them understand why my rate was higher. Now, they lost a month, paid the cheap-o designer to go away, *and* were now investing in my rate.

The experience showed me that self-publishing authors needed help understanding value in book design. It was one of the catalysts for writing this book.

By the way, the author and I moved forward with a collaboration and had a terrific experience working together. The resulting cover is one of my all-time favorites and remains in my portfolio to this day.

Despite this cautionary tale of bargain hunting, I want to make something clear for at least the third time so far in this book: *money is not the magic bullet.* Just as you should beware of low-quality service from budget resources, you should *expect* high-quality service from premium resources. If a designer is asking you to

---

15 I know what you're thinking, and the answer is no, I did not also experience a pang of *schadenfreude*. Of course not. I would never.

invest significantly in a collaboration, they should be able to clearly explain their value up front and unquestionably deliver on it. As such, I'll reinforce something that I've already written and will write many times over: *be sure to vet any design resource before hiring them.* Ultimately, every designer's rate is informed by a unique set of factors, and it's on you to determine what those factors are.

As with any investment you're considering, it behooves you to do your homework, shop around, and ask the right questions.[16] It's the same in design as it is with anything: you should be comfortable with your service provider *before* you sign on to work with them.

> **Pro Tip:** Gather several estimates. The more information you have in front of you, the better you'll be able to compare and evaluate individual resources. Even outlier estimates can be helpful.

What You're *Not* Paying For

When budgeting for design, it's just as helpful to know what *isn't* typically included in the scope of work. Here's a quick list of items you might assume would fall on your designer, but are usually separate services:

→ **Printing:** You'll need to consider a print costs separately. Your designer should be able to recommend a resource. Most authors who are self-publishing will use one of several prominent print-on-demand resources, and in these cases the cost of printing books is effectively passed on to the consumer.[17] However, if

16 We'll explore some of those questions in the next chapter.

17 While traditional offset printing yields the most high-quality product, it is prohibitively expensive for *most* self-publishing authors and would not be worth the investment unless their book is especially sophisticated in its packaging or layout and/or stands to move a significant amount of inventory.

you plan to order a stash of copies for your own use, you'll foot the bill.

→ **Publishing and Distribution Coordination:** If you're self-publishing, don't expect the designer to set up your book project with a publishing vendor. Certain designers are equipped to help you with this step, but it will be an added cost. More commonly, it's a separate focus altogether that the designer will stop short of offering. There are self-publishing coordinators who can help you with this process, and your designer may be able to point you to one.[18]

→ **Latter Editorial Stages:** Back cover copywriting, final proofreading, and indexing are editorial stages that often occur during or after the bulk of the book design has been executed. Still, they are not design deliverables and need to be considered separately, both in terms of budget and timeline. Note that they may also increase the scope of your design services. For example, a proofreader's markup will require your designer to spend time manually updating the layout, and if that wasn't included in the initial scope, you should expect an ad hoc charge for that design time.

→ **Postpublication Revisions/Updates:** Once your designer releases your approved files, any edits thereafter can be billed as additional time. This could include typos

---

18 Of course, you can handle the publishing aspect on your own. Most self-publishing platforms are user-friendly by design, but even so, there are many intricacies along the way that may or may not be intuitive. While the answers are likely a Google search away, many authors would rather hire an expert to help them navigate the process. I did, and it was well worth it.

or other objective errors you might find in the book after it's published.

The good news is that most book designers who have been in the business for any significant amount of time will be able to coach you on these services, as well as introduce you to individuals who can provide them.

3. Where Can I Find a Book Designer?

Broadly speaking, there are three avenues for hiring a book designer: **agencies, crowdsourcing platforms, and independent freelancers.** Each presents benefits and drawbacks, so let's look at them one by one.[19]

Publishing Service Agencies

What Are They? Staffed companies that specialize in editorial, design, publishing, and consultation services

Examples: Creative/design firms, hybrid/vanity publishing houses, marketing agencies

Strengths

→ **Quality:** Agencies generally are formed by individuals who have a vested interest in fielding a talented production team, so you can expect a certain standard of quality, especially from smaller shops where the business stakeholders are senior-level publishing professionals.

→ **Scope of Service:** Agencies can also address a broad scope of needs and may offer bundle pricing to encourage you to concentrate your investments with them. As such, you *could*

19 As the presumptive audience of this book is authors who plan to partner with a professional resource, I will not be discussing the merits of DIY design tools. My official stance: skip 'em unless you want your end result to scream "THIS BOOK WAS SELF-PUBLISHED."

save some money if you have a large enough budget and plan to invest in a wide range of services.

→ **High Bus Factor:** These operations also have a support infrastructure that results in a high "bus factor," meaning that the risk of your project falling off the rails due to a vendor issue is low. If your book designer exits the company or even goes on vacation, you can expect fallback support.

Weaknesses

→ **Cost:** With great scope comes great investment. As such, agencies might be a terrific option if you have a sizable budget *and* are interested in a variety of services. But while turnkey service sounds great, it simply isn't realistic for most independent authors to invest potentially tens of thousands of dollars into publishing services.

→ **Compromises:** If you're partnering with a publisher—traditional or hybrid—you may be forfeiting a percentage of your royalties and may even be compromising some of your rights to the content. This could be worth it to you in exchange for the support and clout that comes with a publisher. (Kinda sounds impressive to say, "I have a call with my publisher today," doesn't it?) It will vary from publisher to publisher, so make sure you understand how any given publishing concern approaches these issues.

→ **Prefab Publishing Teams:** With agencies, you're hiring a preassembled team. While the agency will stand by the quality of their in-house teams, are they necessarily the individuals you would choose to work with? Having served more than a decade as an agency designer, I can tell you that not every author I was paired with was necessarily a philosophical or "work style" match. Some agencies do rely on a freelance bench as opposed to employing in-house designers. This gives them a bit more flexibility to match authors with like-minded designers on an ad hoc basis.

THE BOTTOM LINE: AGENCIES

Consider them if:

You've got ample budget

You'd rather hire a preassembled team than a patchwork of individuals

You are interested in a broad scope of services

Look elsewhere if:

You are hesitant to invest in agency pricing[20]

You are leery of sacrificing rights or royalties (although you may not, depending on the company structure)

You want to assemble your team with individuals you personally vet and hire

---

20 Is it possible that certain agency rates might be less expensive than assembling a team of contractors? Absolutely.

Crowdsourcing Platforms

What Are They? Platforms that connect authors with a pool of freelance designers around the world

Examples: 99Designs, Upwork, Reedsy

Strengths

➡ **Large Talent Pool:** Crowdsourcing platforms are a conduit for design clients and design talent. They're a terrific way to be exposed to a broad spectrum of talent, especially if you don't know where else to look. Design practitioners all over the world lean on these platforms to find work. This includes the author of the book you're currently reading!

➡ **Payment Accountability:** The platforms manage payment, so there is accountability for both the vendor and the client.

➡ **Budget-Friendly:** For authors operating on a budget, crowdsourcing platforms field designers who will work at lower price points.

Weaknesses

➡ **Commissions:** Most of these platforms require the client *and* the service provider to cough up a percentage of the agreed-upon rate, so it's possible you'll pay more than you would on the open market. Of course, plenty of budget providers can be found on crowdsourcing platforms, and even with the commission they might be a cost-friendly option.

> **Pro Tip:** If you come across a designer's platform profile you find appealing, there's nothing preventing you from seeking them out on the open market. Most professional designers have a standalone portfolio site and welcome direct outreach. If a designer is comfortable working with you directly, you would both save money on the platform commissions.

→ **Inflated Rates:** While these platforms are quick to tout their heroism with regard to community building, you must remember that they are cash cow businesses. They take a cut of all projects, and fees tend to creep in for both client and vendor, thus inflating price points. I'm required to use a point of sale service that skims almost 3 percent. After commissions and fees, I give up 13 percent of my payout for any project. As such, I have to increase my estimates to account for that.

→ **Communication Constraints:** Certain platforms limit communication between designers and authors in an effort to prevent off-platform relationships. While I understand the threat it presents to their business model, restricting communication simply does not lend itself to a healthy professional relationship, especially for enterprise-level projects such as book production. As a vendor on a crowdsourcing platform, I am continually reminded that the platform has a vested interest in keeping the author and the designer at an arm's length.

DESIGNECDOTE
Platform Perils

I was commissioned for a job via a crowdsourcing platform by the author of a self-help book. It was his first book, and he was quite nervous about the design process. This is a common and understandable headspace for first-time authors.

Sensing that this client could use a bit of reassurance, I suggested that we schedule a video meeting so I could walk him through my process. He was quick to agree and asked for my email address so he could send me an invitation. I provided it, then received a message about an hour later from a representative of the platform we were using.

The email's text could be best described as a cheerful reprimand: I was informed that providing my email address was a strict no-no. And, yes, it was against their stated rules. (And in fairness, they made that clear during my onboarding call, I just didn't remember.)

However, it was this excerpt from the email that really told the story:

> "In order for us to be able to help both professionals and clients through the process of connecting, contracting and collaborating, we require that all written communication be kept on [platform]."

I found this to be deeply disingenuous. In no way does the platform *actively* provide any help once the connection is established. Once the job's been commissioned, you are unlikely to hear from a platform representative—unless, of course, you send a message that their software registers as a red flag, such as "What's your email address?"

So, how does throttling our communication allow them to "help both professionals and clients"?

The answer, of course, is it doesn't.

They simply don't want the author and designer communicating off-platform because we might be tempted to scurry off and collaborate directly, thus costing them their 10 percent commission. Therefore, "outside" communication is an inherent threat to their business model.

From a business standpoint, it's a reasonable concern. From a user experience standpoint, it's a major drawback.

———————————— ⚓ ————————————

A Note on Design Contests

Certain platforms rely on a contest format, wherein a fleet of designers submit work on spec. This means you only pay for whichever design you choose.

Remember Truth #3: beware of options! The best of a bad set of options is still a bad option, but it will seem appealing by comparison.

This pitfall is actually marketed by the platform as a feature. You're shown dozens of designs from creators the world over and made to feel like the belle of the ball. The problem is that the onus is on *you*, the client, to determine what constitutes functional design. Contests strip away consultation and iteration and simply say, "Pick one."

> **Author's Note:** Perhaps you're thinking, "Of course you're pooh-poohing these methods. *They're your competition!*" This is actually not the case. In my experience, most authors who use low-cost crowdsourcing resources or design contests aren't looking beyond them. In fact, I'm *glad* these platforms are around. They remind consumers of the difference between low cost and high value. I regularly receive inquiries from authors who tell me, "I used [crowdsourcing platform], but it was an awful experience, so I'm looking to invest in a better solution." I'm glad they found me, but I'd much rather they had done so before investing in the inferior solution first. That is, in part, why I wrote this book!

Contests strip away consultation and iteration and simply say, "Pick one."

Do I believe authors can achieve positive results from crowdsourcing platforms? Sure! After all, I am a vendor on one of them, and I like to think I deliver on those projects. But the reason I dug deep in this section is because I think that too many clients default to these solutions without considering their risks. If you determine crowdsourcing is your best course of action for budgetary or other reasons, that's perfectly fine so long as you recognize the threats.

**THE BOTTOM LINE:
CROWDSOURCING PLATFORMS**

Consider them if:

You want convenient and consolidated access
to a large number of providers

You're operating on a budget

You want payment accountability

Look elsewhere if:

You want to avoid commissions and fees

You want to be able to directly and uninhibitedly
communicate with your designer

You are rightfully skeptical of options-based design
solutions (looking at you, design contests!)

Independent Freelancers

What Are They? Sole practitioners who partner directly with clients in need of creative services

Examples: The author of this book

Strengths:

➡ **Flexibility:** Freelance designers can operate itinerantly or out of a home office with relatively low overhead. As they aren't beholden to organizational protocols, they can be adaptable and responsive.

➡ **Entrepreneurial Spirit:** A successful freelancer knows that their best marketing tool is a great client experience, so they'll usually go above and beyond to make sure the client is satisfied.

➡ **Optimal Communication:** You can expect a direct line and, in many cases, a more casual relationship with your freelancer than you would with a designer who is representing a larger entity. Speaking from my own experience, I embrace a personalized and friendly relationship with my clients. We text about the project and generally bond on a personal level. For many authors, this comfort level with their collaborators is important, given the personal nature of their project.

➡ **Network:** Freelancers usually have a robust network of complementary service providers. Need an editor, a proofreader, or a publishing coordinator? Odds are, they can point you in the right direction or even build those services into your agreement and manage them on your behalf.

Weaknesses:

➡ **Low Bus Factor:** The inherent weakness of hiring a freelancer is that there is only one of them. If your freelancer is inundated, it may lead to a slowdown. If they're on vacation or are inca-pacitated somehow, you might be left in the lurch. Of course, most freelancers will have contingencies in place for this. For example, I pay a colleague to be on call for me while I'm away, and—look away, life coaches—I occasionally check my email while on vacation to make sure there are no urgent emergen-cies. While most freelancers keep one eye on the business at all times, it behooves you to dig into these vulnerabilities when you're exploring a collaboration. How do they contend with availability issues? If they're on vacation, do they fully unplug, or will they find time to resolve unexpected snags?

→ **Accountability Risks:** This relates to the previous bullet but warrants its own discussion. Simply put, there is rarely a safety net protecting your relationship with your freelancer. If, for any reason, you experience a lapse in the quality of service, or they simply stop returning your calls or emails . . . what then? There is no employer or entity to whom you can file a complaint. Perhaps you can pursue legal action, but would the juice be worth the squeeze? And after all that, your project is still in purgatory.

→ **Range of Quality:** The term "freelancer" can refer to both a seasoned solopreneur running their own full-time practice *and* a side-hustler without any formal training. There is no barrier of entry to joining the book design industry. There is no board cer-tification or accreditation needed to become a service provider. Don't assume every freelance provider is equally capable. To mitigate the risks presented by this and the aforementioned weaknesses, you must carefully assess your freelance candidates. (Don't worry, the next chapter will show you how.)

THE BOTTOM LINE: FREELANCERS

Consider them if:

You do your best work within the bounds of a personalized, flexible, and casual working relationship

You value communication in a working relationship

You want connections to other freelance resources

Consider looking elsewhere if:

A low bus factor makes you uneasy

You have concerns about accountability

You aren't confident in your ability to discern a dabbler from a seasoned vet

This was a beefy chapter because it might be the most valuable one in the book. There are an overwhelming number of factors to consider when commissioning design work, and so many providers telling you they're doing it better than the rest. You could dice the three larger groups (agencies, crowdsourcing platforms, freelancers) into countless subsets, each with their own nuances and quirks.

My hope is that, by illuminating the three broad categories, I've helpd you determine which one(s) will best address your needs. From there, you can compile a shortlist of candidates. In chapter 4, we'll discuss how to do that.

DESIGN DEBRIEF!
CHAPTER 3: THE HUNT FOR A BOOK DESIGNER

Define Your Investment

Understand you're not buying a product; you're investing in a designer's expertise, process, and ability to collaborate.

Determine a Realistic Budget

"Fast and cheap" usually means "not good."
A meaningful design process takes time and skill,
and that should be reflected in your budget.

Know What You're Not Paying For

Printing, publishing logistics, proofreading, and
postpublication updates are typically outside your
designer's scope (though they might guide or refer you).

Choose Your Avenue

You can hire via agencies, crowdsourcing platforms,
or freelancers—each has pros and cons. Match
the route with your needs and budget.

Avoid Contest-Based Design

Contests and "pick one from many" setups lack
process and strategy. They can be flashy but
often lead to shallow, low-impact designs.

HIRING YOUR DESIGNER

*How to Evaluate, Consider,
and Pick a Winner*

My goal in writing the previous chapter was to help you arrive at an important conclusion: *not all design resources are created equally.* You have options when it comes to the form you'd like your design experience to take. Now you have a clearer idea of what's out there.

But it's also important to recognize that, no matter which avenue you explore—agency, platform, or freelancer— and how much you are willing to invest, one individual designer might yield a radically different experience from the next. This chapter will help you home in on the designer who is right for you.

Why Is One Designer So Different from the Next?

As mentioned in chapter zero, graphic design, as a service industry, is the Wild West. It is not standardized nor does it require any kind of credential. *Anyone* can initiate a career in graphics at the drop of a hat. All one needs is access to design software, which can be downloaded in mere minutes. There is even freeware for those unable to invest in industry-standard design programs. And remember, there is no board certification or official credential a designer must secure. You don't need a college diploma or a high school diploma—heck, you don't need a kindergarten diploma. Just add "Creative Director" to your email signature, and voila—you're in.

Because of these low barriers to entry, it can be tricky for the layperson to distinguish between a high-quality design resource and someone who's just pretending to be one.

This presents another upside of agencies: they've *likely* done the vetting for you. But, as mentioned in chapter 3, this means you're locked into working with whomever they already have on staff. If you elect to pursue a freelancer or find a designer through a crowdsourcing platform, you can whittle your search down to the individual.

When hiring a book designer on the open market, it's critical that you vet them to gain an understanding of the *real* value your candidate stands to provide. This is a step many authors breeze through. They settle on the first option or the lowest bidder. And while cost is always something to consider, it's important that you view value through a more holistic spectrum when reviewing your candidates. Basing your hire on a glimpse of a portfolio and a quick estimate is a risk you don't want to take.

Assessing Your Candidates

Viewing the candidate's portfolio is a no-brainer, but it's only the first step. To understand the real value they'll provide, you must learn about their process, understand their scope of service, review past client experiences, and of course, consider their rates.

Let's take a closer look at each of these factors.

Portfolio

When hiring any sort of creative talent, you'll want to review your candidate's work. Most designers have a portfolio website displaying a collection of their work. Make sure it speaks to your tastes. If they've done a considerable amount of publishing design work, consider the kinds of projects they've worked on. A designer who's specialized in children's book design may not be the perfect fit for your book on advanced data analytics (and vice versa).

When reviewing a design portfolio, here are a few points to consider:

➡ **How much of their portfolio comprises book design?** Remember one of our Three Truths of Hiring a Book Designer from chapter zero: book design is a specialty. Does the designer's portfolio indicate a deep understanding of the ins and outs of the process? Or does it point to a generalist, perhaps showing a single book cover amidst a sea of logos, marketing work, etc.? While I wouldn't go so far as to tell you to beware the second designer, consider that a true specialist might yield more value throughout the process than someone who has only dabbled in book design.

→ **What genres do they have experience with?** The next time you're at a bookstore, have a look at a display of fiction covers. Then check out the nonfiction display. You'll likely notice distinctions in style and tone. Just as you might find a mechanic who specializes in European cars, there are designers who focus on specific genres. Speaking from my own experience, I almost exclusively take on business/nonfiction design. I understand the prevailing styles and design techniques that are functional in that space, and I know how to work with the authors who populate that market. While I wouldn't necessarily turn away an interested fiction author, a book designer who specializes in fiction would be better suited for the project because of their mastery of the nuances of that world. Additionally, they have connections in that space that could prove helpful. Children's books, fantasy, cookbooks—they've all got their practitioners, and finding the right fit for your book will yield the best results.

→ **Does their work resonate with you personally? Do you think it would resonate with your market?** Every designer has a style. You may not be able to describe it, but it should be evident when you browse their portfolio. And if that style resonates with you, it's likely that they'll be more comfortable on the project than a designer who might have to flex into your preferred style. Now, if you love everything about the designer other than their prevailing style, I wouldn't disqualify them. A gifted designer can be a chameleon, but you may want to discuss your vision before hiring them to make sure you (and they) are confident in their ability to execute it.

➡ **Last but not least: Is their design work any good?** This is a deceptively tricky question. What if you aren't confident in your ability to identify strong design work? That's perfectly understandable. The average person simply may not be able to distinguish a great portfolio from an average one. If you question your judgment here, remember that designers with a lackluster portfolio usually fall short in the other areas covered in this section. Your overall impression will point to whether they're a fit.

Identifying an impressive portfolio is a great place to start, but it should be considered a baseline requirement. To that end, you can immediately dismiss candidates whose work doesn't seem like a fit for your project.

The following criteria should more critically factor into your decision to invest in a graphic designer.

Process

A successful book designer has to excel at a lot of things: graphic design (obviously), consultation, communication, project management, and so on. For freelancers, the list would include bookkeeping and business management and other small business functions. It follows that if they're going to squire you through a complex project, they've got to have firm processes in place to manage all these different corners of their workday. Be sure to learn about them as a professional, not just as a designer. It will quickly become clear how capably they can serve you.

Graphic design is a field cluttered with dilettantes and dabblers who know just enough to be dangerous. In some ways, the job title itself has little meaning anymore.

DESIGNECDOTE:
Ceci n'est pas une Graphic Designer

When I was the creative director of a publishing design team, I struck up a conversation with our office administrative assistant. At one point, she mentioned that she took on a bit of graphic design freelance work as a side hustle. I asked what kind of work she did. She told me she loaded photos into an app on her phone that could overlay text and then posted them on social media for a client.

I don't mean to downplay her service, as it's likely she was conducting the exact task that was being asked of her and providing real value to her client. But clearly she is doing something completely different than a design professional who spends all day, every day thinking about book design, living in sophisticated design software, and working with clients across the globe.

But to the consumer, we're both graphic designers.

I share this story for hyperbolic effect. I'm sure you can sniff out the difference between someone who uses an app to overlay text and a sophisticated design professional. But the point is, while "graphic designer" may seem like a title befitting a skilled creative specialist, there's no rule against my app-wielding coworker claiming it.[21] This is why you must take the time to gain an understanding of what your candidates bring to the table.

---

21 This is why, if someone asks what I do for a living, I always say "book designer."

When conducting your search for a book designer, you'll likely be asked to distinguish between candidates with less obvious distinctions in their depth of service. As such, digging into a candidate's process is a great way to separate the wheat from the chaff.

Ahead, you'll find a few points to consider. However, note that it is not imperative that you present these as questions. In fact, doing so might raise a flag with the designer. They might view you as a client who could be a bit overbearing, and thus they may think twice before taking on the project. These are merely factors to be conscious of and consider while you're getting to know your candidate.

➡ **What is the designer's general approach to working with clients?** This is one area that underscores the notion of no two designers being created equally. Every designer approaches creative projects a bit differently. For example, Designer A prefers to send sketches and mock-ups, building the piece out by stages, whereas Designer B prefers to present fully realized concepts. There's not necessarily a right answer, but I would imagine one of these approaches resonates with you more than the other.

Beyond process-related differences, a designer's personality will set the tone for the relationship. Do you prefer someone who has an "all business" disposition? Or would you rather establish a personal connection with the individual? It comes down to your preferences with regard to collaboration. One trick is to evaluate your email correspondence. If you prefer short, concise emails and a businesslike efficiency to communication, you may get aggravated by a designer who begins every email with a meandering life update followed by a detailed overview of their font and color selections.

Conversely, if you think it's important to establish a personal, semicasual relationship with your book designer, you may perceive a red flag in short, objective emails with nary an exclamation point or emoji. Again, there is no wrong answer. Just remember that you'll be working with this individual for weeks or months. Ultimately, you will want to feel comfortable with your collaborator, so ensuring that you can have a frictionless working relationship will go a long way.

➡ **What are their touchpoints as the book is built out?** In other words, when and how often will you, the author, need to be involved? If you like to be involved more or less than they suggest, will the designer flex their approach to accommodate you?

➡ **Is the designer familiar with** *The Chicago Manual of Style* **conventions?** *The Chicago Manual of Style* (commonly referred to as CMoS) is the style guide for book publishing. One of the best ways to help your book avoid the trappings of "self-published" work is to ensure it adheres to CMoS editorial and design standards. This is not to say you can't override certain conventions if you have personal preferences, but a designer who knows CMoS is going to bring a lot of value to your project.

➡ **What is the project lifecycle?** Make sure you understand how the project moves through its phases. It doesn't need to be a deep dive, as long as you understand the cadence of progress. It's helpful to gain understanding of what signifies the formal beginning and end of the collaboration.

➡ **If you're talking to a freelancer, what do you think of their practice?** How long have they been around? How do they manage their caseload? Is their website well-maintained and does it include client testimonials?

➡ **If they're a sole practitioner, do they have contingencies in place for when they're unavailable?** This should be an easy question, but it could have a huge impact on your project if your designer was suddenly unable to work for any reason.

➡ **If book design is a side hustle, how available will the candidate be?** There is nothing fundamentally wrong with hiring someone who moonlights as a book designer. Plenty of very talented designers work full-time jobs, often in a different field. Of course, this will compromise their availability and focus. Back when I was a W2 employee, I would be sure to let potential freelance clients know that I would only be available to work and communicate in the evenings and on weekends, and I couldn't resolve issues during the day. This may have cost me a few jobs, but I think it saved me even more headaches.

Once you've gained a sense of how tight a ship they run, it's time to consider the specifics of your project.

Scope of Service

While it falls on the designer to set expectations, it behooves you to gain a better understanding of the services you stand to receive from each of your candidates. In chapter 2, we discussed what to expect to be included in book design collaborations. Still, some freelancers define scope differently than others.

As such, it's important for you to understand exactly where their scope of service starts and ends so you can gauge value and adjust your budgetary considerations.

Here are some points to consider:

➡ **When the book project is complete, what are the deliverables that will be provided?** Do you receive project files upon completion, or just the prepared printer-ready files?[22]

➡ **How many different cover concepts will you see?** Ask whether you'll see initial designs that are fully realized, as opposed to proofs-of-concept for establishing direction. Consider what you'd find most helpful.

➡ **How flexible are they regarding communication?** For example, would they agree to a rolling meeting schedule? Is there a limit to phone calls and meetings? Are they open to texting?

➡ **What's their approach to revisions, both during the project and after it's finalized?** If you discover errors or typos following the book's publication, how can they be resolved for future printings? Is there a cost related to these corrections?

➡ **What other design services does the designer offer?** For example, you may need marketing collateral or a website.

---

22 See chapter 8 for an expanded discussion of this very subject!

If any of their additional offerings are of interest to you, ask if they offer service bundles at a volume discount.

→ **What** *don't* **they do?** For example, some designers may offer to coordinate directly with a printer; others consider this a publishing coordinator's responsibility. There's no right answer, but it's helpful information for you to know up front.

Reviews, Endorsements, Testimonials

We live in the age of the consumer review, and as such, many book designers are eager to collect endorsements from previous clients as a sales tool. While reviews don't always paint the full picture, they can reveal useful details about a designer's approach. Be sure to look beyond the star ratings. Some reviewers may provide specific commentary that could build a designer's appeal in your mind. For example, if you're worried about poor communication sullying the process, a review that notes the designer's excellent communication skills could move the needle for you.

> **Look beyond the star ratings. Some reviewers may provide specific commentary that could build a designer's appeal in your mind.**

Rates

While all the preceding information is important, let's get to the good stuff: *How much is all of this going to cost?*

After reading chapter 3, you hopefully recognize that rates for the same project will vary drastically across different resources. This is why it's important to understand *why* book designers charge what they do. You might discover that a particular resource is offering a depth or style of service that isn't congruent with your needs. On the other hand, you might recognize value that you hadn't previously considered.

The estimates you receive will be informed by the designer's experience, abilities, process, and philosophy. Designers who operate in a simple and transactional manner may charge less. That's good if you're on a budget, but you may be compromising support and flexibility.

> **Designers who operate in a simple and transactional manner may charge less. That's good if you're on a budget, but you may be compromising support and flexibility.**

Physical location will play a part too. A designer out of San Francisco probably has got steeper expenses than one in Wichita, Kansas. And it's no secret that certain international design labor forces are less expensive, but be aware that these resources may invite frustrations when it comes to communication and accessibility. This is why it's so important to fully understand whom you're partnering with and the value they stand to provide.

DESIGNECDOTE:
A Check Worth Writing

An author reached out to me about a comprehensive book design job. She needed her book jacket designed, the interior layout designed, and the print files converted into an e-book. When I presented her with an estimate, her reaction was a classic case of sticker shock. My rate was several times more than what she expected to invest. But after a healthy discussion and a careful explanation of what she should expect from the process, she took a leap of faith and hired me.

Over the next three months, we worked together to design a beautiful and compelling book that, years later, is still serving its purpose. The collaboration was a joy for both of us, and we remain close to this day.

When she mailed the final payment, she included a note:

> **"I never could have imagined being so happy to write this big of a check for book design, and still feel like I got incredible value!"**

This was powerfully important to me because it's what I try to convey to my authors from the get-go. Yes, there are designers who charge premium rates. But if you hire the right resource, you will feel like it's money well spent.

Of course, the danger here is that a designer could take advantage of authors by overpricing their services, with the hope of creating an artificial perception of value: "They're the most expensive bidder, so they must be good." This is known as the price-quality heuristic.[23] This chapter is meant to serve as a series of checks

---

23 "The Price Quality Heuristic: How it Affects Pricing Psychology." Faster Capital. April 3, 2025. https://fastercapital.com/content/The-Price-Quality-Heuristic--How-it-Affects-Pricing-Psychology.html

and balances that will help you get an understanding of the value a designer stands to provide *before* you agree to their rate. Press your potential designer on all these subjects to get a sense of the bigger picture.

When you're considering a designer's rates, here are a few points to consider:

- → Does the designer bill hourly or by the job?

- → If it's "by the job," how do they determine that amount?

- → What's the payment structure (e.g., 50 percent up front, etc.)?

- → If you're working with the designer directly, what payment methods do they accept?

- → Is there an additional fee for credit card payments?

What Is "Value" in a Design Relationship?

A quick document search tells me I've dropped the "v" word forty-four times thus far, but you still may not have a clear idea of how to identify value[24] in a designer. We talked about portfolio, process, scope, reviews, and rates, but how does it all come together to result in ultimate value? Perhaps spending a few thousand bucks on book design is still inconceivable to you. After all, design is a squishy thing to invest in. "Does a $2,000 book cover really look ten times better than a $200 cover?"

While I'd argue, in most cases, it does, this is admittedly a subjective stance. But hopefully by now you've gathered that

---

24 And there's forty-five.

the value of the designer extends far beyond the quality of their creative output.

Let's take a look at "perceived value" vs. "real value." The chart below depicts what the layperson might reasonably assume captures a book designer's value:

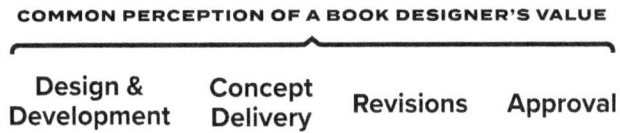

Simple, right? *The designer makes it, you review it, the designer revises it, you approve it.*

The practical portion of the process *could* be radically distilled into these essential steps. However, it would be an oversimplification of what a full-service book designer's value really encompasses.

Let's zoom out a bit:

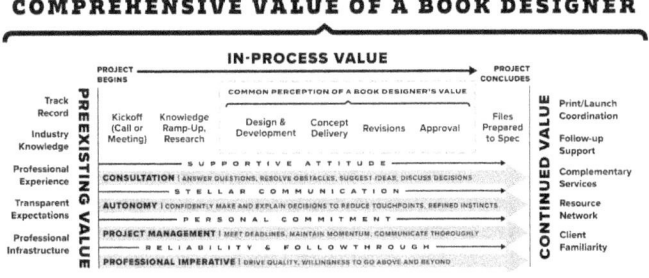

Presented here for effect. See enlarged graphic on the next page.

This diagram paints a far more detailed and accurate picture of what a competent designer brings to the table. Remember, you're investing in much more than a product.

COMPREHENSIVE VALUE OF A BOOK DESIGNER

IN-PROCESS VALUE

PROJECT BEGINS

PROJECT CONCLUDES

COMMON PERCEPTION OF A BOOK DESIGNER'S VALUE

| Kickoff (Call or Meeting) | Knowledge Ramp-Up, Research | Design & Development | Concept Delivery | Revisions | Approval | Files Prepared to Spec |

SUPPORTIVE ATTITUDE

CONSULTATION | ANSWER QUESTIONS, RESOLVE OBSTACLES, SUGGEST IDEAS, DISCUSS DECISIONS

STELLAR COMMUNICATION

AUTONOMY | CONFIDENTLY MAKE AND EXPLAIN DECISIONS TO REDUCE TOUCHPOINTS, REFINED INSTINCTS

PERSONAL COMMITMENT

PROJECT MANAGEMENT | MEET DEADLINES, MAINTAIN MOMENTUM, COMMUNICATE THOROUGHLY

RELIABILITY & FOLLOWTHROUGH

PROFESSIONAL IMPERATIVE | DRIVE QUALITY, WILLINGNESS TO GO ABOVE AND BEYOND

PREEXISTING VALUE

- Track Record
- Industry Knowledge
- Professional Experience
- Transparent Expectations
- Professional Infrastructure

CONTINUED VALUE

- Print/Launch Coordination
- Follow-up Support
- Complementary Services
- Resource Network
- Client Familiarity

The four arrows running across the bottom are the most underappreciated yet important characteristics of a designer. **Consultation, autonomy, project management,** and **professional imperative** aren't sexy terms, but they encompass so much of what drives a designer's value. Let's take a look at each.

1. Consultation

You're investing in *expertise*. You should be able to talk through ideas and receive guidance from your designer. When I was a young and inexperienced book designer, I'd always do exactly what the author asked of me, no matter how misguided the suggestion. "You want two guys in suits shaking hands on the cover of your business book? You got it!" An experienced designer knows how to pinpoint the intent of a less-than-advisable directive and suggest alternative solutions that satisfy the client and yield great results.

2. Autonomy

While a cut-rate designer may know their way around the software, it's possible that they are not going to operate with the degree of autonomy of a more tenured designer. For example, they might litter your inbox with emails to solicit your opinion on minutia. I've found that authors appreciate when I use my best judgment and defend my decisions if and when necessary. This reduces touchpoints and makes for a smoother progression through the process.

The other side of that coin is equally as important. Inexperienced designers may avoid asking important questions that warrant the author's input or just not recognize when a client may need a courtesy check-in. Don't underestimate the value of a designer who has a feel for a comfortable rate of interaction.

3. Project Management

Unless you're working with a publisher or an agency, you probably don't have a project manager who is responsible for keeping you and the designer on task. Even if you do hire one, it should still fall to the designer to establish deadlines, communicate expectations, and maintain project momentum. I can't tell you how often I hear, "My last designer would take five days to get back to me after each email. I felt like I was a burden every time I reached out." This is unacceptable but is often the case with bargain design resources. Momentum is especially critical for any book project, and your designer should embrace their role in maintaining it.

4. Professional Imperative

You could reframe this as, "How does the designer carry themself when you're not watching?" Do they take shortcuts if it's something the author won't notice, or do they spend a few extra minutes to adhere to best practices? Do they maintain a standard of high quality, even if the author seems to be okay with "good enough"? Do they go above and beyond expectations? Do they have an obvious sense of pride in their work? Are they accountable for their errors?

When I talk to young designers, I often remind them of the importance of professional imperative. The truth is, many clients are not equipped to recognize great work. Some might not even know the difference between "good" and "below average" work. The onus is often on you, the designer, to advocate for your work and make it better than it needs to be. A seasoned designer has the confidence to push back, to engage in discussion, and to value a client's input while steering them clear of disaster.

As the author, you are hiring the designer for their expertise, and it is only through a strong professional imperative that they will ensure this expertise is reflected in your final product.

Making the Hire

Congratulations! You've done your due diligence, asked the right questions, reviewed proposals, and are ready to make an investment in a book designer.

While this represents a major milestone, I needn't dig too deeply into what happens now. Your resource will guide you on all aspects of the collaboration, including whatever needs to happen to formalize the initial engagement.

In the interest of providing a general expectation, here's how each of the three primary types of book design resource might get the ball rolling:

1. **Hiring an Agency:** Once you inform the agency of your desire to move forward, it's likely they will draw up a formal agreement. You'll be asked to review and sign the contract; they may even schedule a call to go over it with you to answer any questions and solidify your expectations. Once signed, you'll provide a form of payment that they'll keep on file. The agency will draft payments based on whatever cadence is dictated in your agreement (monthly payments, milestone-based, etc.). The specifics might vary from agency to agency, but generally speaking you can expect the most intake structure from an agency, especially if they have a full-blown sales team.

2. **Hiring a Designer via a Crowdsourcing Platform:** The actual hire will be as simple as clicking a big fat "Accept

Collaboration" button (or something similar). Generally, these collaborations roll up into boilerplate legal protections, so by accepting the collaboration you're agreeing to those terms. You'll then have to add payment information. From there, it's up to you and your designer to forge ahead.

3. **Hiring an Independent Freelancer:** Of the three categories of book design resource, this one is likely to be the most variable across different providers. Some freelancers are fine with a casual relationship where contracts aren't involved. Others (myself included) do insist that a contract is in place before the project starts. I prefer to formalize my collaborations in this way because it gives us both peace of mind, accountability, and a record of information. A freelancer's approach to payment might also be less formal and consistent across different vendors, but in most cases book designers are happy to use standard payment apps like Venmo, Zelle, and PayPal. Checks and credit cards are also commonly accepted forms. Freelancers may charge a small fee to accept credit cards since they'll likely be giving up a percentage to their point-of-sale software. Once a deposit is paid (assuming there is one) then it's off to the races. The freelancer you've partnered with will advise you on next steps. The process unfolds from there!

There's much to digest in this chapter, but don't let it bog you down. I encourage you to read it a time or two before beginning your search, but don't feel like you're undermining your chances at a winning book design if you don't conduct a weeks-long analysis of your various options.

The reason I belabor the search is because so many authors fail to make even the most basic considerations. The path of least resistance can be all too attractive. A solid morning of research and outreach could make all the difference.

Here is how to approach the search, in simple terms:

1. Make a short list of a few book design resources.

2. Dig into their website and reviews. Make sure you have a good sense of who they are.

3. Submit an inquiry to any design resource you're interested in (even if it's only one).

4. Explore a collaboration, keeping in mind some of the key points outlined in this chapter.

The goal of this chapter is to urge you to dig below the surface of your search. Remember the importance of this moment: you are partnering with a person or resource who is going to be responsible for shaping your all-important message into a visual form that will represent you before a large audience. Don't underestimate the importance of devoting an appropriate amount of time, energy, and budget to ensure you get the right person in that seat. You'll thank yourself later.

DESIGN DEBRIEF!
CHAPTER 4: HIRING YOUR DESIGNER

Graphic Design Is Unregulated

Anyone can call themselves a designer. Portfolios fail
to tell the whole story. You need to understand the
designer's process, communication, and mindset.

Evaluate the Portfolio Strategically

Look for specialization in book design and alignment with your
genre and audience. Pretty doesn't always mean purposeful.

Understand Their Process

Ask how they collaborate, how revisions work,
and what the communication cadence is. A good
designer will have clear, thoughtful answers.

Compatibility Matters

Think about your working style. Do you want frequent
updates or a more hands-off process? Choose
a designer whose vibe matches your own.

Red Flags to Watch For

Vague process, restrictive policies, inflexibility,
or lack of publishing knowledge—any of these
can spell trouble in a collaboration.

PART 2

THE ANATOMY OF BOOK DESIGN

Your largest battle has been won: you've found your dream designer.

I devoted the first half of this book to the importance of finding the right book designer because I believe it is the single most critical—and overlooked—factor in the book design phase of your publishing journey.

Hypothetically, if you *had* to bail on my book at this point, you'd be in great shape.

Still there?

Good on you! The truth is, many authors sell short the importance of their role in the book design process. You may not be responsible for the execution, but your buy-in and participation is critical.

My definition of success in a design project is the point when the client and designer are both immensely proud of the result. There is often a push and pull required to get there, which is why active collaboration between author and designer is so important. Sometimes, the initial concepts a designer presents are miles away from what the author is envisioning. That's not necessarily a bad thing, but it does underscore the importance of iteration and discussion in a design process.

And it points to how important an author's input is to the book design process. Let's say I send you a cover design, and the entirety of your reaction is, "I don't like it; can you show me something else?" I am now left guessing as to what my strategy is going forward. But a great designer recognizes that a rejection is merely an opportunity. A great designer will *not* get emotional or defensive but will instead say, "No problem. Let's talk about what isn't working, what *is* working, and how we can address what is missing."

Remember, your involvement is a luxury you *get* to have as a self-publishing author. Traditionally-published authors often have little to no say when it comes to the book's packaging. Embrace the fact that you get to work with your designer to arrive at a solution that looks professionally crafted and that you're proud to call your own. This will empower you to go confidently into the marketplace.

Ahead, we'll discuss the different stages of book design and how you, as the author, can best serve the collaboration. We'll also discuss how you might *hurt* it. I'll provide a few case studies and get you up to speed on some jargon that may help you speak your designer's language. By the end of this section, you should have a general sense of the flow of a book design project and a better understanding of how to plug into it.

Read on!

THE FRONT COVER

Casting the Star of the Show

The face. The front door. The gateway.

Pick your favorite metaphor for illustrating the powerful role of your book's front cover. Whichever your preference, we book designers recognize it as the star of the show and the design element that gets authors the most excited. For many, the cover establishes a visual language that will continue throughout the interior of the book and could even blossom into a brand that becomes larger than the book itself.

I won't spend any more words selling you on the importance of the front cover, because you're probably on board already. In fact, it's possible that some of you are *so* eager to dive into the front cover that you flipped right to this chapter. (If you did, be sure to go back and read part 1—even if you've got a vision, hiring a great designer is the key to a great cover!)

But since you need no further convincing, let's talk about what the front cover actually does ... and what it doesn't do.

A front cover's job is fourfold:

➡ **It must compel.** Imagine a person scanning a robust book display. Is there a visual gravity to the design that will earn you an extra split-second's worth of review? Will the reader think, "This author looks like a credible resource who has something interesting to say"?

➡ **It must intrigue.** To intrigue via a book cover design is to capture the author's voice and broader message without overwhelming the design with text or visual messaging. Movie poster designers do an especially good job with this. The best posters capture the spirit of a two-and-a-half-hour blockbuster in a single static design, leaving the viewer to think, "Oh, this looks interesting..." I believe a great book cover will do the same justice to its content. But remember, you're only cracking the door. Don't make the mistake of cramming content onto your cover with the hope of telling the full story. You'll never do it, and you'll inundate the viewer.

➡ **It must inform ... lightly.** Especially for nonfiction books, the cover should help your audience understand its topic. However, I believe it's a bit of an overrated function of the front cover. The back cover copy should do the informational heavy lifting. The front cover needs only to tease the subject and propose a measure of value. It should speak to the right audience and position key words and phrases in such a way that will introduce the subject (but more importantly, intrigue and compel). Remember, your cover is not a flyer for the book, where all information needs to be consolidated in one place. The front cover is meant to prompt a specific behavior in the viewer—flip the book over or click the link. Simply put: find out what this is all about.

→ **It must endure.** If you ask me to ascribe one quality to successful book design, it would be this. Trends come and go, but great design will persevere. Even if something looks like it was born "of an era," it should still stand up after that era is bygone. Endurance in design has less to do with style than it does with composition and messaging. I believe this is true in other media (fashion, music, film, etc.).

As a corollary to this list, I'll present you with one thing that is *not* the job of the cover: selling books. Call it a CYA if you must, but I believe it. So does Chip Kidd, one of the great book designers of our time, who asserts that great book covers provoke exploration.[25] At the end of the day, a great cover alone won't sell your book. It sets off a chain of behaviors that may result in a sale, but great design is meant to attract attention and elicit a response. In a strange way, the back cover is more critical to a book sale than the front. (Worry not—we'll touch on back covers in chapter 6!)

> **A great cover alone won't sell your book. It sets off a chain of behaviors meant to attract attention and elicit a response.**

25 Chip Kidd. "Designing books is no laughing matter. OK, it is." TED Talk. March 2012. https://www.ted.com/talks/chip_kidd_designing_books_is_no_laughing_matter_ok_it_is?subtitle=en

In any case, excellent cover work can position a book favorably in the mind of a reader, regardless of their interest in the subject. Conversely, a shoddy cover can dash a reader's impression of a book—and its author—without their reading a single word of it. For an author who intends to use their book as a lead generation or credibility tool, low-caliber design might not only cause a book to be overlooked but in fact *repel* the market. The stakes are high.

Is an event organizer going to invest thousands in a keynote speaker whose book cover looks like a throwaway? Will a potential client view you as an invaluable resource if your cover's haphazardly slapped together?

You know the answer.

How You Can Help the Process

An outstanding cover design is the result of combining two powerful forces: the author's subject expertise and the designer's skill for visual communication. As such, you need to recognize your importance to the process. Do not make the mistake of assuming your role is limited to writing a check or swiping a credit card and then waiting for a freshly designed book to arrive in your inbox.

Here are some ways you can help your design professional arrive at some dazzling solutions:

1. Do Your Homework

Prepare your mind for the process. Start thinking about book design as a consumer. Go to the bookstore and snap photos of covers that stand out to you. Conduct the same exercise for covers you *don't* like. Compile four or five of each, and shoot them over to your designer. If you can, explain what you like and don't like about the respective collections. If you have trouble putting this into words, don't worry—your designer should be able to find the commonalities.

Don't stop at covers either. If you are drawn to specific elements of interior layouts—say, chapter title pages or pull quotes—share these with the designer as well. (Better to draw these examples from your home library, though. Photographing the inside of unpurchased books might not be the best look!)

2. Assemble a Brief

A design brief is an overview of the project that will provide high-level information and direction that will set the table for the designer. It can include nuts-and-bolts information such as your preferred color palette and font families, but it also tradition- ally includes project information that is not design related. What feelings or reactions do you want the cover design to evoke? And don't underestimate the negative approach. Sometimes it's easier to tell a designer what you *don't* want than what you do.

If this sounds arduous, worry not: your designer will likely provide you with a questionnaire that prompts you for information about the design.[26] And if you are given an opportunity like this, my advice is not to breeze through it. Set aside ten minutes and really focus on your answers. As a designer, I can tell you nothing is more valuable at the top of the process than a thoughtfully completed questionnaire.

---

26 If they don't, they should. Tell them to put one together for you and use it going forward! They'll thank you later.

3. Keep an Open Mind

While it's fine, understandable, and even advisable to approach the process with a vision, it's equally important to be open to something completely different. Sometimes, your vision is informed by the existing market. "All books about (my subject) are green, so my book should be green." Maybe. But what if yours is blue or hot pink? It'll stand on its own. It'll serve as a pattern interrupt to your market, who may have similar preconceptions as to what a book on your subject *should* look like.

DESIGNECDOTE:
Looking (for Answers) in the Other Direction

A mentor of mine once advised considering the most illogical solution to a creative problem. As an example, let's say your book is about elephants. Logic dictates you need to show an elephant on the cover of that book.

Do you? Let's say you *had* to design the elephant book without actually showing an elephant. What's an alternate solution that might intrigue, compel, and inform the audience?

➡ An elephant's shadow, cast over the title

➡ An elephant's footprint, housing the title

➡ The title is visually textured with an elephant's skin

➡ A pair of tusks and a trunk coming down from the top of the page. (Wait...we're showing part of the elephant! Is this cheating? Maybe! But the thought exercise got us there.)

➡ A brick wall with an elephant-shaped hole in it, surrounded by rubble.

The point I'm making is all of these ideas express something unique, suggest the "elephant" subject matter, but do not feature a full and clear depiction of an elephant. Whether or not you use the ideas, **counterintuitive ideation** is an exercise that you may encourage your designer to undertake ... assuming they aren't on it already!

———————————————— 🐘 ————————————————

4. Provide Meaningful Feedback

Design feedback is one of the most important contributions you can provide throughout this process. Productively responding to feedback is a skill possessed by any capable designer. It's akin to echolocation. We bounce ideas off of you and use your responses to gear our approach going forward. Our hope is that the work we show you is the right general direction, but we also know it may spur some helpful reactions. To provide "helpful feedback," dig into the specifics. What do you like in particular? What don't you like? Consider fonts, colors, and other visual components of the cover. Don't be shy—this is your designer's chance to take the design from good to great!

> **Example of helpful feedback:** "Overall, I like the direction. The title font is great, but I think the readability of the subtitle could be improved. My main concern is the color scheme, which feels a bit off. It's too tropical. I want it to be more metropolitan and a little more serious. I do like the textured effect of the background—can we bring that out more?"

> **Example of unhelpful feedback:** "It's not bad. Anything else can we do to make it better?"

How You Can Hurt the Process

Just as readily as your contributions can support your collaboration, they can also detract from it. Here are some behaviors and tactics that may seem helpful but actually might be moving the needle in the wrong direction.

1. Outsourcing Your Opinions

"I asked a few people what they thought and ..."

"I shared it on LinkedIn and Facebook ..."

"My nephew is a design student; here's what he said ..."

Words that send shudders down the spine of even the most hardened design professional. We wince at the thought of our meticulous creations being torn asunder via loose-knit committee feedback.

Before I continue on, a caveat: I am quite sensitive to the headspace of the independent author.[27] They're tasked with signing off on hundreds of decisions over the course of a book's production lifecycle, and not one of them will have a more visible impact than the front cover. It is understandable for this pressure to be compounded by a lack of confidence as it relates to evaluating design. If solicited for an opinion you don't feel confident providing, it's a perfectly natural impulse to turn to your network for a form of moral support.

It is not my intention to completely dissuade you from the exercise, but rather to help you understand its real value. So

27 After all, I am one.

let's start here: *social media feedback is not tantamount to scientifically gathered data, and it can often cause more harm than good.*

You need not spend much time on social media to recognize that some users are more active than others—some, a *lot* more active. When you post your concepts and ask for feedback, there are those who are predisposed to rush forth with critiques. Some will present them defiantly—perhaps hyperbolically—and for all the world to see.

But who is to say that their feedback is viable or worth considering at all? Anecdotal evidence alert, but I haven't noticed a strong correlation between "frequent social media commenters" and "thoughtful, nuanced commentary."

And what about those insightful individuals who *don't* feel compelled to comment? What about passive peacemakers who might have worthwhile input but would rather not upset the apple cart? What about those fascinating folks who—*gasp*—aren't social media users?

When soliciting feedback on social media, responses will be powerfully biased toward individuals who are two things: extremely online and demonstrably opinionated. What's worse, there may not even be alignment in those opinions, but rather the fashion in which they are conveyed.

> **Social media responses will be powerfully biased toward individuals who are extremely online and demonstrably opinionated.**

"You'd be *crazy* not to pick Concept 1!" says Commenter A. "What? Concept 1 doesn't make any sense," responds Commenter B. Now what?

The biggest problem, in my mind, is this: when you solicit feedback on *concepts*—which, by definition, are works in progress—it's impossible for your network to evaluate speculative designs through the same lens as they would the final product. This is because your concepts lack a powerful and underrated ingredient: *activation.*

When you solicit opinions on works in progress, a dynamic is established, and you are on the business end of it. You place all authority with the reviewer, no matter who they are.

But when you change the context from "What do you think of these speculative designs?" to "Behold, the final cover of my upcoming book!" the dynamic changes, and so will the reactions. Some of your would-be critics will instead become celebrants.

DESIGNECDOTE:
The Opinion That Matters Most

Years ago, when I was a young staff designer at a publishing house, I was assigned to an author who could best be described as the ultimate Type A personality.

He was a very successful business leader. Calls had to be scheduled through his receptionist. He only emailed in short, solitary sentences. In some ways, he was a dream collaborator: he communicated efficiently, detested micro-management, and valued autonomy in his team. But he was an intimidating presence to a young professional like me.

Prior to our kickoff call, I was supplied with his intake questionnaire. Unsurprisingly, it was light on information. When it was time for our call, his executive assistant patched me through.

The call lasted all of two minutes. His only direction? "Just make it freaking[28] awesome." Seriously, that's what he said, and we were off the call fifteen seconds later.

So I hit the drawing board, armed with but a few notes and his reverberant one-liner. I pulled together a trio of cover concepts and emailed them to the author.

A week passed. No response. Do I dare nudge a man like this? I decided to give him the weekend. When I logged into my email on Monday, I saw his response:

"George: I posted the covers on Facebook." This was followed by a link to the post. That was it.

I clicked the link. There, beneath the post that showed my three cover concepts, more than a hundred comments engaged in a rhetorical battle royale. I saw everything from "I don't like any of them," to a person who told him to let their nephew design it, to a subthread that had devolved into a political flame war.

I returned to his email, unsure of how to respond. So I replied in the only way that felt logical: "Lots of varying opinions! I'm curious: What do you think?"

The author replied minutes later. "I like the second one. Go with it." And we did.

From that day on, "What do you think?" has been my standard line when confronted with social media results. This not only protects me from becoming mired in unproductive committee bickering but reminds the author that they—not a random assemblage of platform users—are the ultimate stakeholder.

---

28 He did not say "freaking."

Perhaps, despite all my rhetorical handwringing, you still feel compelled to conduct an informal social media poll. That's perfectly fine.

I will reemphasize that it is a deeply unscientific exercise, and you needn't feel beholden to any feedback you receive, especially if it counteracts your instincts. I firmly believe that if 99 percent of your respondents prefer cover one, but your gut is telling you to go with cover two, then, buddy, go with cover two.

Furthermore, you and your designer should make a point to actively consider alternatives to the prevailing feedback rather than solely relying on the most popular or widely refrained opinions. Conducting a social media poll for feedback can be beneficial—or at least not counterproductive—*if* approached with a mindful consideration of the potential pitfalls.

Here's the compromise I'll leave you with:

1. *Skip the social media polls.*

2. Check in with a small handful of trusted colleagues in a direct and private manner.

3. Consider their feedback before you embrace it or take it at face value.

4. Discuss it with your designer, and place the highest value on your mutual decisions.

2. Overcooking Your Feedback

While I do encourage you to provide thorough feedback, there is such a thing as overdoing it. The first form that takes is tiptoeing around direct criticism because you're worried about hurting your designer's feelings. While I do appreciate the headspace, I can tell you that, as a designer, I'd far prefer a concise response with some hard-hitting critiques over a long-form, ego-stroking email that tucks criticism between the folds of generic praise. Providing criticism is not always easy for the sweet and empathetic among us, but just remember that it is a means to an end.

One of the best feedback emails I received in recent memory was structured in a really helpful and motivating way. The author opened with a short expression of gratitude and excitement. She followed with five things she loved about the designs and five *specific* things that either weren't working for her or she'd like me to try on the next pass. Within a few days, we had our final cover.

It was a balanced approach that was motivating and created a clear path forward. Of course, your scenario might warrant its own version of this—it helped that one of the designs I sent her was quite close to the mark—but using the "what works / what doesn't work / what you could try going forward" approach could provide a helpful structure.

Glossary

Author's Note: *I have included a few glossaries containing terms that you may encounter as you move through the design process. Don't worry too much about mastering the terminology, but a loose familiarity with the concepts could help streamline your communication. It'll also help you sound smart at parties.*

Bleed

This refers to graphic elements that interact with the edge of a page. This is a concern for printers because any product that has a bleeding element must be prepared a bit differently. Bleed can be an effective tool because it suggests something happening *off* the page.

Center of Visual Interest (CVI)[29]

The graphic element that looms the largest on a page. Every great design has one. With book covers, it will likely be the title or an image of some kind.

Colorway

Traditionally used in product design, it refers to the different color schemes in which a product might be available. It has been adopted in the graphic design world to be interchangeable with "color scheme," likely because it sounds a bit more sophisticated. (That's only a guess, but let's just say I know a lot of designers.)

Emboss

A press treatment wherein a specified portion of the cover stock is physically raised for effect. As of this writing, embossing is not available on the digital press. However, designers can digitally create the effect using design software.

Finish

This refers to the physical "feel" of the cover. In the world of self-publishing, there are two predominant finishes: gloss and matte laminate. In simplest terms, gloss is "slick and shiny" while matte is "smooth and flat." Personally, I prefer matte finishes for just about any cover, although certain designs warrant a gloss finish.

Foil Stamping

A press treatment wherein a layer of shiny, foil finish is applied to a specified portion of the cover stock. Again, it's not available on the digital press, but designers can simulate it using graphic elements.

---

29 This is not an official term, but I include it as an homage. I learned it many years ago from the individual who introduced me to the world of graphic design: my high school journalism advisor, Tammy Watkins. I owe her my livelihood. While she was more of a writer than a designer, as a veteran of the newsroom she knew a lot about page layout. One of the terms she taught us was center of visual interest, or CVI. Including it here is mainly a tribute to her, but I do think it's a terrific term!

Spot UV

A press treatment wherein a gloss coating is applied to a specific portion of the cover stock. As with the other treatments, it's not currently available through the digital press but can be simulated using graphic elements or color gradients.

Print Resolution

You've heard it before: "I need a hi-res photo." But what exactly does that mean? It refers to the pixel density of an image, which is measured in DPI (dots per inch). Printers usually require images to be 300 DPI at full size in order to ensure high-quality reproduction. Conversely, your screen can reproduce a quality image at only 72 PPI—or pixels per inch. (While the terms DPI and PPI are not purely interchangeable, you can generally think of them similarly.) The headline is this: your printer needs a much larger image file than your screen does. A full-sized photo that looks crisp on your screen will only reproduce at about 25 percent that size in print quality.

Trim Size

A fancy way of describing the dimensions of the cover of your book. The most common print-on-demand trim sizes for business books and novels are 6" x 9", 5.5" x 8.5"[30] and 5" x 8". Large coffee table books like cookbooks may have more unique sizes, as they are mainly printed through traditional presses that can accommodate custom sizes.

Title Lockup

The graphical presentation of your title.

---

30 Example of a 5.5" x 8.5" book: *Don't Make It Look Self-Published*!

Vector vs. Raster

These are graphic format terms that are important to grasp. And while they're relatively simple concepts, they can be difficult to explain, especially since confusing exceptions lurk behind the broader definitions.

The most rudimentary explanation: *vectors are made out of shapes, while rasters are made out of pixels.* A computer can enlarge vectors without loss of quality, because vectors are composed of shapes that can be represented with mathematical data.

Meanwhile, a raster image is composed of a fixed number of tiny, colorful building blocks called pixels. When a raster image is enlarged, your computer has to create new pixels to account for the extra building blocks required to compose the larger image. This is why images get blurry or "pixelated" when they are digitally enlarged. Your computer is only so good at guessing the nature of the new pixels it needs to create.

With vectors, you have the advantage of scalability. They are by nature simpler graphics. Think of your company's logo. It was almost certainly created as a vector. Letters that comprise a font are technically vectors too. That's why letters on a billboard reproduce at the same quality as letters on a business card. They're just shapes that a computer can digitally enlarge without sacrificing quality. The tradeoff is that vectors are typically capable of less visual complexity than raster images.

Here's where it gets tricky. Let's say I take your company's logo and convert it to a JPG. Even though it still *looks* like a vector, the vector "information" has been flattened into pixels, and so it's now a raster image. It's kind of like a clay pot getting fired into pottery. It may still look like clay, but you can't remold it.

Thoroughly confused? Fear not. Thankfully, you read part 1 of this book and have hired an outstanding designer who can worry about all this stuff so you don't have to.

DESIGN DEBRIEF!
CHAPTER 5: THE FRONT COVER

The Cover Is Your Book's Ambassador

It's the first (and sometimes only) chance to grab your reader's attention. It must communicate professionalism, genre, and value instantly.

Great Covers Provoke a Response

A cover should signal what the book is and who it's for. It's a tool, not just decoration. This mainly applies to nonfiction, but even more artful and abstract fiction covers should be designed with the viewer's reaction in mind.

Your Input Is Valuable—but Shouldn't Overpower

While your vision matters, trust your designer to discover solutions you hadn't considered. Embrace collaboration, not control.

Beware of Outsourcing Opinions

Opening up your process to social media polls and other outside voices can create more problems than it solves.

Strive to Provide Functional Feedback

Win the revisions stage by arming your designer with specific, constructive feedback; this will empower them to take your concepts from good to great.

THE REST OF
THE COVER

Back, Spine, and Beyond!

Congratulations: your book has its dazzling front cover. Thanks to your thoughtfully executed search for the perfect design partner and your seamless contribution to the process, you've arrived at a timeless solution.

But wait … there's more! If you intend to publish your book in print, the exterior design process doesn't end at the left edge of your book's front cover. You've got at least two other slabs of visual real estate to consider: the back cover, the spine, and beyond.

While these elements don't warrant quite as much creative focus as the front cover (diva that she is), we must not overlook their value to the overall product. In fact, the back cover is arguably the most critical cover component in terms of actually getting a potential reader to open your book.

Let's take a look at each of these components.

Back Cover

Imagine that you're on vacation in a city you're unfamiliar with. On the hunt for some lunch, you walk by a snazzy-looking storefront with cool signage and modern decor. Intrigued, you step in and wait patiently to be greeted by a host or server. Minutes pass. No one. After waiting a reasonable amount of time, you shrug, walk out, and continue your search.

This tragic scenario is analogous to a book with a faulty back cover. Your attention is captured, but a lack of engagement sends you looking elsewhere. Okay, the metaphor isn't airtight, but both scenarios fail at a critical juncture: converting *interest* into *adoption*. That is what a functional back cover does.

In the previous chapter, I talked about the jobs of a front cover: to intrigue, compel, and inform, roughly in order of importance. While each of these factors also matters to back cover composition, I believe the order should be inverted: inform, compel, intrigue. Information is now at the forefront. This is your chance to really tell the reader what the book is about and to present its value.

> **Author's Note:** Writing the back cover text is an *editorial service*. This is text that will need to be furnished by your editor or someone you commission specifically for this purpose. If you're confident in your abilities, you can try writing it yourself (perhaps with an assist from Uncle A.I.) But I offer the same advice that I did for design: don't underestimate the value of an experienced specialist who can work with you to fine-tune the message.

The designer's role in maximizing each of these factors is critical, even though they aren't writing the content. Book designers understand how to hierarchically treat back cover text and visuals in a way that will efficiently and powerfully impact the reader.

What to Include on Your Back Cover

Although it's primarily an editorial question, the back cover content is so closely linked with its design that it's worth detailing here.

The first thing worth mentioning is this: there is no one way to do it. The specific makeup of your back cover copy is a strategic decision. Which mix of content will compel your readers to take the all-important step of opening your book?

Ahead, I'll detail the common elements found on a back cover, but know that it's rare that all are included on a single back cover, especially on a paperback book. There's only so much real estate, and the worst thing you can do is overwhelm your reader. Less is assuredly more. You don't need to tell the whole story. Remember: inform, compel, intrigue. Present value to the reader—both yours and the book's—without wandering into the weeds.

Let's look at a few elements that are commonly found on the back cover of nonfiction books:

Book Synopsis / Summary / Blurb

This is a concise and compelling summary of the book's main ideas, themes, and key takeaways. Highlight the most interesting or unique aspects of the content to grab the reader's attention.

Typically, a set of bullets will be housed below the synopsis. The bullets detail some of the specific nuggets of value the reader will find within the pages.

Finally, a short conclusion-style sentence or paragraph will often follow the bulleted list.

Author Biography

A short author biography should emphasize the author's expertise or qualifications in the subject matter. Mention your relevant credentials, previous works, or notable achievements. This should be more concise and have a different tone than your manuscript's "About the Author" section, which can be more personal.

Author Photo

Most authors elect to include a professional yet approachable author photo to help readers connect with the person behind the book. For business nonfiction authors, there's added importance to this if you're intending to use your book to generate leads or in-person opportunities like keynote speeches or workshops. Positioning yourself as an authority figure will assign to you an aura of credibility and esteem in the eyes of your readers.

Endorsements

Testimonials from credible peers or individuals familiar to your market can supercharge your back cover. External validation is one of the most powerful forces in modern behavioral persuasion. Do you zip down to the reviews section of any product you're considering purchasing? Me too. The description will always tell the best story, but what *other* people are saying about it will assign some humanity to the experience. This is why endorsements are so critical.

I routinely design back covers that *only* include endorsements. Many authors believe that a batch of credible endorsements will build trust for the potential reader, which outpaces the utility of a synopsis and bio. For example, here's a completely made-up testimonial for my book:

> "*Don't Make It Look Self-Published* is a must-read for any independent author searching for a book design solution. The value of having an experienced book designer walk you through the

most critical considerations of commissioning book design cannot be overstated. Boasting nearly two decades of book design experience, George provides simple, clear, and action-able advice that will help you get the most out of your design collaboration."

—Nigel Von Arthaus, award-winning author and designer

Within that quote, you learn something about the book (synopsis!) and the author (bio!) while leveraging the power of validation through endorsement.

What about endorsements on the front cover? It's quite common to see a short, punchy quote appear on the front cover. Often, this is done if the individual providing the endorsement is especially notable. But even if they aren't, you might still elect to include an endorsement on your front cover if you think it's powerful enough to compel your readers to flip the book over.

Call to Action (CTA)

Many authors choose to include a QR code, social media handles, or their website in order to encourage readers to take action or learn more.

Imprint Logo

Even if you are self-publishing, you'll create an *imprint* under which the book is published. You'll likely establish this imprint when you purchase your ISBNs. It's as simple as choosing a name—mine is called Olinova Press, a portmanteau of my grandmothers' maiden names. It's wise to have a logomark created for your imprint, as it conveys credibility. You can commission a logo designer for this, or your book designer may be willing to craft something simple for a small fee.

Bar Code and Price

First thing's first: I'm going to save you twenty-five dollars. Do not buy a bar code. Ever. Certain publishing service providers will upsell you with little add-ons like bar codes or QR codes. Don't do it! Your designer should have the tools to create these for free. (If they don't, email me, and I'll create one for you.)

With that out of the way, your designer will include a bar code for the back cover of your book. It will include your ISBN and your price.[31]

Pricing your book is equal parts art and science. You'll want to find a sweet spot that ensures a pleasing royalty for you and conveys value to your readers but is within or near the expectations of the market. While this matter strays outside design considerations, it's likely your designer can weigh in. If you have a publishing coach or coordinator, they'll be able to provide guidance as well. Once your page count is finalized, the print costs can be determined, which will help you decide on a reasonable price point.

Back Cover Word Count

While we've established back cover copywriting is an editorial concern, the word count will impact the design. Although the back cover is an important opportunity to share information to as-yet-committed readers, you must avoid overdoing it. A visually noisy and information-flooded back cover could suggest a similarly overwhelming reading experience waiting within. It's important to

---

31 One school of thought for authors who rely on "back of the room" sales discourages including the book's price on the bar code or anywhere on the jacket, in case you want to be able to dynamically price it. These authors may wish to sell their books at different price points in different appearances, and thus would not want to advertise a specific price. This is a judgment call. I included the price on my book because most traditionally-published books do and thus it is in line with the mantra implied by this book's title, but you may choose to skip it if you think it will be limiting. Either way, it will not be the decision that makes or breaks your book's success.

find a sweet spot that presents authors with valuable and compelling information without inundating them.

> **A visually noisy and information-flooded back cover could suggest a similarly overwhelming reading experience waiting within.**

So, how many words should it be?

Advice will vary depending on your resource. I coach my authors to keep paperback word counts at 250 words or fewer. If your book has a dust jacket, you've obviously got more room to work with, so you might double that total across all panels of the cover.

If you're visually inclined, you can ask your designer to mock up a back cover layout using placeholder text. You can then build the copy based on prescribed word counts, which can be a helpful way to keep you (or your copywriter) in check as you compose the text.

Your designer should feel comfortable requesting a truncated version of the back cover copy, if they determine the layout is suffering. Just as it was with the front cover, the back cover design process should be an iterative buildout. Don't feel confined to the first approach you see.

The Spine

Ode to the Spine
By George B. Stevens

A book and its jacket,
So oft intertwined,
But what are its covers
Without a good Spine?

For the front and the back,
Be they paper or leather,
Without our friend Spine
Simply won't stay together.

Your cover's a wonder,
But do tell yourself:
It's likely the Spine
That you'll see on the shelf.

So let's raise a toast
To this strip of design
That binds us together;
Three cheers for the Spine!

Hang on—is the spine so important that it warrants an *ode*?

Perhaps the poem was a bit much. Seriously: don't let the spine keep you up at night.

That said, it certainly shouldn't be overlooked as a design element. After all, as the ode suggests, the spine is the portion of your book that will most commonly be visible. Why wouldn't you want it to serve as a visual draw?

The spine is an interesting canvas. It's long and relatively skinny. To give you an idea, it takes a 500-page book[32] to yield an inch of spine width. A 200-page book yields a spine that's less than half an inch thick. This book's spine is 0.464", if you're curious.

Thankfully, you read part 1 of this book and thus have hired a skilled designer who understands how to leverage contrast and font styles in a way that will maximize readability.

Shift Happens

When printing your book via on-demand services (the destiny of most self-publishing authors), there are a pair of constraints that must be acknowledged, both of which can be blamed on *shift*. Shift is exactly what it sounds like: Sometimes when you have a big machine churning out thousands of books, slight mechanical shifts occur that can cause alignment inconsistencies from copy to copy. This is just the reality of the process.

Offset printing (the traditional method) is much more precise, but unless you're willing to shell out for it, digital shift is something you have to live with. In my experience, nowhere is it more noticeable than the spine. The good news is that it's usually untraceable when reviewing a single copy. But if you line up twenty digitally printed copies of the same book, it's likely that you'll notice the spine text jumping around by a few millimeters from copy to copy. (If that's frustrating to think about, just know that every book designer agrees!)

Because shift does indeed happen, here are a couple ground rules of digitally printed spines:

---

32 A 500-page 6"x9" paperback book, printed through IngramSpark, on standard stock, would have a 1.005" spine.

➡ **Avoid text that hugs too closely to the margin.** This is true of any design canvas but is rarely more critical than on a book's spine. Thankfully, digital templates include a "spine safe" area to prevent any truly close calls, but I tend to play it even a bit safer than they suggest. The closer your spine text is to the edge, the more noticeable shift issues will be.

➡ **Beware spine backgrounds that contrast with the cover background.** More simply put, it's a good idea for a white cover to have a white spine or for a patterned cover to continue its pattern around the back. This is unfortunate, because contrasting colors between spine and cover create a really cool dimensional effect when viewed from an angle, but it's risky with a digital print run. If your cover is black and your spine is yellow, there's a risk of any given copy showing a razor-thin strip of yellow on the black front cover. That will look like a mistake.

How to Make the Most of Your Spine

Despite the limitations of on-demand printing, the spine is still an opportunity to reinforce your book's visual language. The fonts, colors, and even graphical elements from the cover should be built into the spine layout. Let's take a look at some of the content that might populate the spine:

➡ **Book Title:** A no-brainer! Make sure your book's title is bold and beautiful on your spine.

➡ **Author Name:** Another obvious one. Let 'em know who wrote it.

Last name or full name? *A common question I'm asked when it comes to spines is, "Should I list out my full name, or is my last name enough?" Once again, I give you that most obnoxious of answers: it depends. My belief is that the book title's readability is paramount, so going with your last name is perfectly sufficient if you don't have adequate space for it in full.*

➡ **Imprint Logo:** Most books include some sort of logomark or emblem. You've probably seen the logos for Penguin Books, Simon & Schuster, and other big five publishers emblazoned on spines. We talked about the imprint logo in the back cover section, so if you had one created for that purpose, this is another opportunity to show it off. While it's not required, I do believe it will invite credibility to your publication since most readers expect to see it. By the way, the spine's depiction of this logo may be a simplified version. It may just show the graphical portion of the logo without text, for example.

➡ **Graphical Element**: I look for opportunities to infuse some graphical element from the cover to add a bit of visual flare to the spine. For example, if the cover uses hand-drawn arrows, I'll place one on the cover pointing toward the title. If you have large visual elements that bleed off the edge of the cover (e.g., a climbing vine), you might have it wrap off the front cover, across the spine, and onto the back cover.

Generally speaking, that's it. I have seen subtitles included on thicker spines, but in most cases I believe this to be unnecessary. Just remember: *readability is king!* Think about how your spine will look in a line of books. Will yours stand out? Does a scanning eye have a reason to stop on yours?

> Think about how your spine will look in a line of books. Will yours stand out? Does a scanning eye have a reason to stop on yours?

I'll underscore the prevailing message of the second act of this book: work with your designer to help you arrive at the best solution. Don't feel like you need to have all the answers, or a strong opinion at all. When it comes to the book's spine, your designer is the chiropractor.

Bonus Section: Dust Jackets!

If you're reading this: hey there, Fancypants.[33] You've elected to print a book with a dust jacket and thus will need a bit of extra attention when it comes to your book jacket.

The dust jacket is a sheet of paper that wraps around the boards of a hardcase book. Major releases are often first printed in "hardcover dust jacket" format before eventually being rolled out in paperback. Sometimes this happens concurrently, or even in reverse—this book's dust jacketed version released months after the paperback—but the dust jacketed version is usually considered to be the premium format. This invites a unique consideration for the jacket layout, since there is more real estate to work with.

---

33 Please listen to the Ween song of the same name to get a sense of how I delivered that line.

A (Very) Brief History of Dust Jackets

In its earliest form, the dust jacket was essentially a gift wrapper that fully enclosed the case-bound book, and it was expected to be discarded after purchase. The first dust jackets that were meant to remain a part of the book after its purchase emerged in the early 1800s. According to Brendan Sherar, founder of Biblio:

> The modern-style dust jacket was first introduced in the 1830s . . . (and) could remain on the book when it was opened, providing protection for volumes even as they were read.[34]

So, there you have it. Dust jackets: nothing new. (I told you this was a *brief* history, right?)

What Goes on the Flaps

The flaps are the perfect landing spot for the author bio and photo. Often, the synopsis will find its way to the other flap, leaving the back cover wide open for endorsements. I'd say this is the most common preference of my nonfiction authors, which further underscores the value of endorsements.

The flaps can also comfortably house other bits of information to reduce clutter on the back cover. Below is an nonexhaustive list of content candidates for your flap:

➡ author bio and photo
➡ synopsis
➡ price
➡ publisher name

34 Brendan Sherar. "A Brief History of the Dust Jacket." *Biblio*. Aaccessed July 28. 2025. https://www.biblio.com/book-collecting/basics/a-brief-history-of-the-dust-jacket/?srsltid=AfmBOoqOrtwBEPLZCfrPQsV8b4M35YDi4kOQqgSQf4i78v6toybXtjZe

- book, author, or publisher website
- contact information
- QR code

There's no one right answer, but as is the theme of this self-publishing journey, you don't have to arrive at your answer on your own. Consult with your designer and jacket copywriter about the most strategically sound approach for your book.

What Lies Beneath

What about the hardcase book beneath your jacket? As of this writing, there are three options that are offered by the most prominent print-on-demand resources:

1. Plain gray cloth case, book title generically stamped onto the spine.

2. Plain blue cloth case, book title generically stamped onto the spine.

3. Fully printed case.

If you choose the third option, it means that you will need your designer to create a fully designed file used for the case under the jacket. Keep in mind this is a more expensive option, but many authors go this route because it isn't so generic. Furthermore, if the reader loses the dust jacket, the book will still retain its design appeal. The design may be a repeat of what's on the full jacket, or it may be a simplified version with a blank back cover.

Don't let this chapter overwhelm you. The good news is that your designer (and your cover copywriter) can handle most of these decisions, or at least provide counsel and recommendations. All of the considerations detailed in this chapter are addressed consistently by your publishing experts. Their experience, fused with their understanding of your project, will point them to the best solutions.

DESIGN DEBRIEF!
CHAPTER 6: THE REST OF THE COVER

Back Cover = Second Impression

After grabbing attention with the front, the back cover must seal the deal. It provides context, credibility, and a clear call to action.

Author Bio and Testimonials Matter

These elements build trust. Keep bios concise and relevant and testimonials targeted toward your audience.

Copywriting Is Design

The words on your back cover are just as important as the visuals. Cluttered copy undermines your message.

Bar Code and Publisher Details

Functional elements like bar codes, ISBNs, and logos should be present but unobtrusive.

It's a Package, Not Just a Picture

The front, spine, and back must work together cohesively, not as separate pieces. Think of the cover as a single story told in three parts.

THE INTERIOR LAYOUT
*It's What's on the Inside
That Counts*

*Author's Note: For most of this chapter, the interior layout refers to the
print version of the book. We'll discuss the e-book at the end of the chapter.*

**You might be surprised to learn that many people
I've encountered don't intuitively think of the
book's interior pages as a design concern.** Or perhaps
you are not surprised, because you are one of them. And if you are,
don't feel bad. Given the shadow cast by the book's front cover,
the inside is at best dismissed as an afterthought and sometimes
completely disregarded.

The reality is that the interior layout merits considerable
design attention. In fact, in most cases the interior is a *more*
intensive and time-consuming design undertaking than the jacket.
This is especially true for cookbooks, children's books, textbooks,
or any publication that requires unique layout considerations for
each page. But even for text-forward publications like business

books and self-help resources, interior layout design requires a high degree of detail awareness, technical know-how, and, yes, creative drive to achieve exceptional results.

Why Does the Interior Layout Matter?

Whether or not they are consciously aware of it, readers who sit down with your book are partaking in a user experience. How would you like them to describe it? Perhaps you'd prefer descriptors like *enriching, educational, personal,* or *calming.*

What if a reader described their experience with your book as *frustrating, arduous, uncomfortable,* or *repelling?* Probably not the language you'd like to be associated with your work. Yet this is the risk an author takes when they underestimate the value of a great interior layout.

Much like dining at a restaurant, flying an airline, or visiting the dentist, reading a physical book is a four-dimensional sensory experience that warrants a thoughtful, holistic approach by the author to ensure the end user associates positively with it. As such, a great manuscript will suffer without a great layout treatment.

Consider the three comparative examples I provided previously (restaurant, airline, dentist). Businesses in each of these industries cannot thrive solely on the quality of their core service. An airline that leads the nation in safety rating and on-schedule flights can still earn a bad reputation if the flight attendants are notoriously unfriendly, the meals are repulsive, or the cabins are hot. Everything must be accounted for in order to ensure a great user experience.

This is especially true of business and nonfiction books in which hierarchical information is being presented to the reader. For a book that seeks to drive a desired behavior in its readership—

whether it's adopting a new lifestyle, embracing a philosophy, investing in an idea, whatever—the manner in which the information is presented can affect the way the reader perceives it.

That's no great revelation either. It applies to just about any form of communication. If you want someone to invest $50,000 into a venture, would you meekly mumble your pitch while staring at your feet, or would you show them a dazzling presentation? Similarly, you want *your* book's message to feel important. It should convey authority and gravitas. A stunning interior layout treatment will do exactly this.

> **You want your book to convey authority and gravitas. A stunning interior layout treatment will do exactly this.**

How You Can Help the Process

As with the cover, you should expect your designer to understand and handle all the technical aspects and inject visual flare into the work. But there are ways you can contribute to their efforts. As is the case with every phase of the book design process, your command of the book's message is an important asset for the book designer. As such, providing the layout designer with cues and signals will help them recognize opportunities for supercharging the book's interior design. Here are some suggestions:

1. Make Use of Styles

In Microsoft Word and in Google Docs, there is a Styles panel/tool that allows you to assign specific treatments to any given style. The default style is "Normal"—this is ideal for your main body text. But perhaps your book has multiple levels of subheading. In order to signal that hierarchy to your designer, assign respective "Heading" styles to them, like the following:

- ➡ Chapter Title: Heading 1
- ➡ Section Subtitle: Heading 2
- ➡ Section Sub-Subtitle: Heading 3

Doing this will help your designer in a few ways. First, the styles provide a mapping system to clearly convey your titling conventions. Additionally, the assigned styles in your word processing software will actually translate to the layout file, which will allow your designer to directly swap preassigned styles with those they've created. By the way, don't worry about the aesthetics of the styles—using program defaults is fine. Your layout designer will handle the visual stuff during the interior design process.

One final note on this matter: your editor *should* be on top of this. If they aren't planning on using Heading Styles, I'd encourage them to do so.

2. Provide Cues to Your Designer

Don't be shy about leaving comments in the manuscript for your designer for any content-related visual touches that you'd like them to include. Highlight the relevant text, and provide any helpful context you can. While your designer will familiarize themselves with your content, you'll be able to flag opportunities for visual flare better than anyone. Here are a few examples:

- → "Treat this text as a pull quote."

- → "This section should be treated as a sidebar—consider putting it in a gray box or distinguishing it in some way."

- → "Add a few lines beneath this question to allow the reader to write in their answer."

As with the previous section, your editor should look out for these moments and add comments accordingly, but it's worth keeping in the front of your mind as well.

3. Commission a Proofread

This advice is brought to you by my two decades of experience in book production. I've been involved, on some level, with more than a thousand book projects. I can confidently tell you that, no matter how thoroughly a book was edited in the leadup to design, flaws always sneak through. Both the trained human eye and the digital grammar sentinels are incapable of capturing every last issue. When a manuscript is typeset, you'll perceive things anew, including errors that somehow camouflaged themselves during the composition phase. A great proofreader will be on the hunt not only for grammatical errors but also inconsistencies, omissions, etc.

> **No matter how thoroughly a book was edited in the leadup to design, flaws always sneak through.**

While a proofread is yet another expense, it is a critical safeguard. In fact, if you could only afford one editorial pass, I *could* make an argument for it being a proofread. It's that important. If you hire a great designer (and of course you will, thanks to this book!), they will likely be able to connect you with an excellent proofreader.

4. Make Peace with Your Manuscript

Think of layout as a design phase, *not* an editorial phase. When you deliver your manuscript to the designer for its interior layout treatment, embrace the fact that your work, as a composer, is complete. (And remember chapter 1: *celebrate!*)

Yes, inevitably you will wish you had phrased something differently or included a section on this or that.[35] *Every* creator goes through this. But the worst thing you can do is try to rearchitect the book when construction is already underway. Do your due diligence during the editorial stages, have faith in the work you put in, and let the process unfold as intended. In the next section, I'll expand on what can go wrong if you don't.

> **Do your due diligence during the editorial stages, have faith in the work you put in, and let the process unfold as intended.**

---

35 There are cases where a world event or technological advance might call for adjusting or adding to your manuscript *after* the book has been published so it doesn't seem obsolete. Self-publishing platforms do allow for adjusting book files, quickly and cheaply, without necessarily needing to republish the book. If you deem it critical, your designer can work with you to update the layout. Keep in mind this will require adjustments to the structure of the layout, new cover templates, and a reconversion of the e-book, all of which will require an investment.

How You Can Hurt the Process

1. Post Layout Rewrites

Below I will recount a scenario that is an aggregate of many actual accounts to which I've been privy as a book layout designer.

> You, the author, open your browser to an unread email titled "Book layout for review." Excitement wells within you. You're downright giddy to see your manuscript in its final form. You scroll through the PDF, beaming with pride and fulfillment: it has chapter titles, running headers, a copyright page . . . At long last, *it looks like a book!*
>
> Now wait a minute. That third paragraph on page 24— could it be worded more clearly? Shoot, maybe the whole chapter needs recalibrating. In fact, should it be split into *two* chapters? Of course, that will mean adding some extra copy to flesh out each new chapter.
>
> You know what? Better read every chapter and see if anything else needs shoring up. You know it's the last minute, but you want to get it right!

While this scenario is the sort of thing that sends shivers down the spine of any production-minded graphic designer, I concede that it is an understandable impulse. When the finality of publishing sets in, "panic tweaking" becomes a temptation for any author. While the desire to improve your manuscript should not be discouraged, the problem is twofold:

1. Late-stage content changes are often done in haste,
    without the depth of consideration you afforded
    during early editorial stages.

2. Adjusting the content of a completed layout can have
    severe impacts on its structure. This could lead to
    scope adjustments that will drive up your costs and
    extend the timeline.

Each of these issues is a trap, for distinct reasons. Speaking to the
first point, it's easy to mistake "new" for "better." I get it: You've
read your manuscript a zillion times. The words feel familiar, even
predictable, and less exciting. There is a temptation to spice up
your content with fresh language. Just remember, any new content
at this point will be raw, unrefined, and not have been subject to
editorial considerations that ensure a tight, cohesive manuscript.

Anecdotal Evidence Alert! As a creator, I can relate to the
allure of newness when familiarity sets in. Having designed
thousands of book covers and layouts, and recorded more than
a hundred songs, and written one book, there's something satisfying about a fresh element cutting through a known flavor. But
I can also tell you I've regretted many late-stage additions and
tweaks. If you feel the impulse to adjust, ask yourself: "Will this
change *objectively* make it better?" If you cannot confidently say
yes, leave it be.

Now let's talk about the structural implication. Reworking
your manuscript after the layout has been completed is like recon-
figuring the floor plan of a new home after it's been constructed.
To reverse course, the builders would have to unwire electrical,
tear out drywall, and so on. It will take lots of time and lots of
money. Such is the case with a book's layout. This is why authors

must make a point to conduct their "final final" manuscript review prior to passing it off to the designer.

An unfortunate truth that drives the desire to fiddle: some authors don't afford the proper depth of focus during the editorial phases. They only dial in their focus when there is a sense of urgency to get it right. "I'm supposed to publish next week? I'd better actually read this thing!" (I'd imagine there's an overlap here with last-minute Christmas shoppers.) If you are prone to this sort of thinking, now is the time for self-awareness! Don't save your critical eye for the last minute. In fact, you should think of the manuscript handoff—not your press date—as your last crack at it.

I acknowledge that this is a much easier prospect for some authors than others. Some of us have trouble letting go of our creations. Others bash out content and move on to the next thing without a second thought.[36] For those of you who are tempted to tinker, here's a reality check: you'll *always* wish you'd done something differently, no matter how perfect you think you have it. I promise you, a year after the book comes out, you'll reread it and recognize things you wish you would have handled differently.

Every creator (including the writer of your favorite book, movie, or album) experiences this phenomenon. Accept that your book is a snapshot of the hard work you put in up to this point. There are always second editions! A book that's mired in publishing purgatory isn't doing much good for anyone—not for the author or its potential readers. Be thorough during the editorial process, and it will yield confidence and peace during the layout review.

---

36 If this is you, you'll want to read the upcoming section, "Skipping a Proofread."

Together, let's recite the "Author's Acceptance Creed":

Today, my book is the best one I am capable of.
I created it with passion, intent, and confidence.
It is not perfect.
Tomorrow, I will wish I'd changed something.
But today, I am glad I didn't.
I will be saved by Saint Second Edition.

2. Index Assumptions

Upon delivering their layout, I have had authors ask, as an after-thought, "Oh, will you create the index?" as if they were asking me to add their middle initial to the title page.

There is no easy button for an index. This must be understood.

Indexes[37] are, simply put, a bit of a bear. Indexing is such a specialized and time-intensive task that there are professionals who do it exclusively. It's a step that should be factored in during the planning and budgeting stage of your book journey. Your designer should know that your book will be indexed *before* they bid on the job because it will impact their process and scope of work.

> **Your designer should know that your book will be indexed before they bid on the job because it will impact their process and scope of work.**

---

37 Yes, I know the preferred plural of index is "indices," but "indexes" is also ac-ceptable per *The Chicago Manual of Style* so I chose not to muddy the waters with arcane grammatical turns!

As such, consider whether you *need* an index before you commission one. For certain books, they are a helpful tool that adds value for the reader. However, I am of the opinion that most books don't need one.

3. Skipping a Proofread

Yes, I already mentioned the proofread in the "How You Can Help" section, but I'm doubling down on this one because I think it's that important.

I will reinforce what I wrote in that section: *every book has errors.* Every last one of them. I actually found a typo nestled in the heart of John Steinbeck's *The Grapes of Wrath.* Whether the author himself was responsible, or it was a data entry issue by the bookmakers, is unclear. But the point remains that one of the great American novels, which was issued by a major traditional publisher and was no doubt subject to severe editorial scrutiny, has at least one error in it. So does the book you're currently reading. And—yes—so does the one that you're writing.

Readers will generally be forgiving when a book contains a few spare hiccups but will find it hard to look past a book that's rife with typos and consistency issues. Often, the books of those that skip the step of proofreading fall into the latter category. And it follows that *those* works are far more likely to be recognized by the reader as substandard. Remember, your reader will tie the author's value to that which they perceive of the book.

Also remember that proofreaders are doing more than looking for spelling and grammar errors. They're scouring the layout for inconsistencies, attribution errors, and various "gremlins" that somehow slipped past multiple rounds of editing. Would you believe that I've seen a proofreader flag the book's title written incorrectly in the preface? In this case, the book's title had slightly shifted at the eleventh hour, and no one remember that the preface text included the old title. Thankfully, the proofreader spotted it and an embarrassing error was avoided.

Yes, proofreading is an added expense. Your proofreader's fee will correlate with the word count of your book, and it's likely your designer will have to bill you for the time it takes to manually execute the edits. At this point, you've invested handsomely in the book, and you may feel hesitant to put another cent into it. But I encourage you to find the budget to fortify your efforts. Scour your couch cushions if you have to. You'll be glad you did. It never fails that the proofread captures something glaring, even in the most carefully edited manuscripts. Don't assume your book is immune to this trap.

Glossary

Front Matter

The information that is presented prior to the book's formal start (the introduction, usually). Listed in the most standard order, here's what it might consist of:

Testimonials/Endorsements

A collection of quotes in support of the book or author, usually placed at the immediate front of the book.

Half Title and Full Title Pages

There are two title pages at the front of the book. The half title page should only show the main title. The full title page should show your main title, subtitle, author name(s), and imprint logo. Visually, these pages usually mimic the typography of the front cover.

Copyright Page

A "fine print" page, showing legal and publishing information. This usually includes the book's title, author, copyright year, ISBN information, legal disclaimers, and so on. Copyright pages vary between publishers and authors. Your designer can show you examples, or you can examine your own library.

Dedication

A sentence or short paragraph indicating to whom the book is dedicated. (Example: "To the many mentors and teachers who have inspired me. Thank you for showing me the way.")

Table of Contents

A paginated list of sections and chapters. Sometimes subheadings and other content subdivisions are included.

List of Figures

This is a table of contents for the figures. Usually only included in technical resources.

Foreword

An introductory message meant to lend credibility to the book's message or author, usually written by someone who is not the author themselves. (Note the spelling: foreword, not forward! Just remember that it comes before the words and you'll never get it wrong again.)

Preface

This is a message from the author to the reader. It's usually more personal in tone, capturing the author's "why." (Remember the Author Onion?)

Introduction

Technically the introduction is not considered part of the front matter—in fact, it is when roman numeration gives way to standard numeration—but I include it because I think it's important to distinguish it from the previous two entries. An introduction sets the table for the content of the book. It lays out the themes and message and may include a chapter outline.

Not every book needs every front matter section. I've designed plenty of books without a foreword or preface, for example. It's up to you to decide what's most important to your product.

Back Matter

Content that follows the body of the book. Listed in the most standard order, here's what it might consist of:

Conclusion, Epilogue, Afterword

These are three distinct sections, but for our purposes, I'll lump them together because it's unlikely you'll need all of them, especially in a nonfiction book. The conclusion is the back matter's answer to the introduction. It's how you holistically tie up the book's message. You might review key points or share lessons or words of encouragement to your readers. Epilogues and afterwords are more common in works of fiction. The former is considered part of the narrative, providing a glimpse into what happens after the book's main narrative concludes. I do see them in memoirs but rarely if ever in books by subject matter experts. The afterword comes from the author directly, usually a final note with which to leave the reader.

Appendix

Compilation of tables, figures, resources, etc. that appear throughout the book, and/or supplemental materials that may not have found a natural place in the main text.

Acknowledgments

This is a fleshed-out section where you thank anyone and everyone who might have helped or impacted your book in some way. This probably includes shoutouts to your family, colleagues, editors, and of course your beloved designer.

> **NOTE:** *The Chicago Manual of Style* prefers acknowledgments as a back matter section, per an update in their 18th edition released in 2024 (prior to then, they preferred it as a front matter section.) While acknowledgements can also be placed in the front matter, I tend to agree with their updated suggestion.

Endnotes

Resources that are referenced throughout the book; often used instead of footnotes.

Glossary

List and definitions of key terminology that is pertinent to the book's subject. You're currently reading one!

About the Author

A short biography of the author, sometimes accompanied by a photo. You may already have a short biography on your book cover. Whereas that should be brief and focused on credibility, the about the author section can be longer and might contain more personal interest details. For example, if you are a world champion kazoo player, it's better to mention that in the about the author section than on your back cover snippet.[38]

References/Bibliography
A compilation of works that were referenced to support the development of the book.

Resources
A list of websites, books, videos, or other media that the reader may find useful.

Index
Paginated list of key terms, phrases, and concepts that appear throughout the book. Often developed by an indexing professional separate from your designer.

Contact Page
Pertinent contact information. May include email, mailing address, website, phone number, etc.

Call to Action
A page that encourages the reader to take some sort of next step: visiting a website, joining a mailing list, etc.

As with the front matter, not all sections are needed. Your editor can help determine which are key for your manuscript.

Leading
A typographical term for "line spacing," i.e. the space between lines of text. (By the way, it rhymes with "*bedding*.")

---

38 Unless, of course, your book is about kazoo mastery, in which case it should be the first thing you mention on the cover.

Pull Quote

A line from the body text that is reproduced in a styled and enlarged fashion, serving as a visual element within the flow of the book.

Recto and Verso[39]

The right and left pages, respectively.

A Brief Section about the E-book

I initially budgeted a full chapter for this subject but ultimately decided to reduce it to a subsection. Why? Because, frankly, there isn't a ton of input *you* will be asked to provide on this compared to the other design stages. Furthermore, it's a gray area as to whether e-book production is a "book design" concern, as it relates to the focus of this book.

Still, it behooves you to understand what exactly an e-book is, how you should think about it as a product, and how well your print book may (or may not) translate to its digital edition.

An e-book is a digital version of your book, embedded with interactive touches like live links and a drop-down table of contents, known as a navigation TOC. Think of it like your book has been transformed into a website. In fact, your e-book is supported by the same core files as a website (HTML and CSS). Every part of your book—content and visual touches—is translated to code, which e-readers are designed to support.

Types of E-books

There are two kinds of e-books: **reflowable** and **fixed layout**.

---

39 If there's ever a Pixar film made about the publishing industry, these would be terrific character names.

What's the difference? Your intuition is probably correct: reflowable e-books adjust their content based on the user's settings. You can increase text size or rotate your device; whatever you do, the book's content will adapt and reflow to encourage an optimal reading experience. Most e-books adhere to this format.

Fixed layout e-books, on the other hand, feature locked content. They could be reasonably compared to a PDF file. Unlike their reflowable counterparts, the content cannot shift or be controlled in any way by the reader, other than zooming in or out proportionally. Fixed layout e-books are primarily used for books that rely heavily on visuals to convey their message: cookbooks, children's books, graphic novels, and so on. Books that do not meet various qualifications cannot be submitted to most distributors as fixed layout e-books.

File Formats

The standard e-book file format is the mighty EPUB, supported by most e-readers. Reflowable EPUBs can support much of the visual flavor of the print book. Quite notably, however, Kindle readers convert EPUB files to a proprietary format. What this means is that much of the EPUB's flare will be stripped away and replaced with generic styling. So don't be surprised if you open your book on a Kindle and much of its unique flavor has been stripped out.

What Will (and Will Not) Translate

This section will speak specifically to reflowable e-books, since they are the most common and user-friendly e-book format. They're also the format that will less faithfully translate from the print book, so it's important you understand what will not translate.

What Will Translate

➡ **Text Content:** Worry not—all your text will port over directly from the print version.

➡ **Images:** All inline images will export cleanly. Keep in mind that certain e-readers do not support color, so if your print book is in color, you may want to consider reimagining infographics or other visuals that rely on color to convey specific information. Also consider that more images make for a larger e-book file in terms of file size. Your EPUB royalty may shrink based on the size of your EPUB file. This is a bigger concern with fixed layout EPUBs.

➡ **Links:** Any link in your book will become live in an EPUB format, allowing users to access websites, social links, and so on.

What Won't Translate

➡ **Page Breaks (as they exist in the print version):** When text reflows due to adjusted user settings, pages might break differently. While certain pages will still break intentionally—chapter title pages, for example, will still begin on a dedicated "page"—the main body text will simply break wherever it runs out of room on your screen. As such, it's advisable to flag anywhere you reference the physical location of content (i.e., "see the graphic on the next page") because these references might become obsolete. I suggest you simply label your visuals with figure numbers, which will allow you to reference them without relying on page locations (i.e. "see Figure 4.1").

➡ **Page Numbers:** Similarly, page numbers will be adjusted based on the user settings. So you'll need to account for any page references in the book (i.e. "see page 72 for tips on organizing your finances"). Your e-book specialist will be able to replace that page number with a clickable cross-reference.

➡ **Fonts (in many cases):** Some fonts will embed while some won't. Certain e-book conversion purveyors and services will require the fonts from a print file in order to embed them into the e-book. Technically, they would need to acquire a license for doing so. Your book designer can't simply pass along fonts for which they only own a print license. Furthermore, many designers use cloud-based fonts these days, so embedding them into an e-book may not be workable. As such, generic versions may have to be substituted. Furthermore, the Kindle version of your book will be automatically stripped of custom fonts and replaced with preset styles. Don't get too attached!

Will My Book Designer Convert the E-book?

The short answer is, "Maybe." Some book designers are cross-trained in e-book conversion. Some do not consider it part of their focus, requiring you to commission it separately. Speaking of my own process, I do offer e-book conversion, but I rely on an external vendor who specializes in coding to finalize the file.

It's important to gain an understanding of how your book design resource factors e-book conversion into their scope prior to going under contract.

Dotting the "i" in Book Design

The revisions have been made. The e-book has been converted. Your designer has prepared each of the files you'll need.

It's time to push the publish button.

Amidst all the excitement and anticipation, there is probably a thick fog of finality hanging around you. This audacious project you've spent years planning, thinking about, building, and refining is about to be gifted over to the world.

It's a weighty moment, and one that can paralyze authors. But the fact that you approached the design process (both the hire and the collaboration) in a measured, thoughtful, and deliberate manner should imbue you with the confidence and pride necessary to carry you across the threshold.

Publishing a book is impressive. Publishing a *good* book is a rarity. You accomplished the latter. For the rest of your days, "author" is a part of your identity. Heck, it'll be in your obituary. (Dark, yes, but if that doesn't spell the magnitude of your accomplishment, I don't know what will.)

Go forth and publish! And remember that this is not the end of the journey. You're just getting started. The launch day will come and go; it's up to you what happens next. Other bright, shiny objects will beckon, but don't forget about all the time, effort, and resources you poured into making it great. Your book will take you as far as you want it to.

Self-publishing isn't just about the method of book production. It's about your freedom to stand on the platform you created. The world's waiting, and they'll be lucky to have a book like yours. Go get 'em.

DESIGN DEBRIEF!
CHAPTER 7: THE INTERIOR LAYOUT

Interior Design = Reader Experience

The layout should be clear, inviting, and genre appropriate. It affects readability, pacing, and professionalism.

There's More Than You Think

Interior design includes font choices, margins, chapter openers, image placement, headers, footers, and more.

Small Decisions = Big Impact

Thoughtful formatting of elements like pull quotes, lists, and sidebars can elevate your manuscript into a pro-level reading experience.

The E-book Is Its Own Animal

Certain visual components of the print book will translate to the electronic form; others will not.

Finalize with Pride and Confidence

Approving the book for print is a big moment, but it's a lot easier when you're proud of the process that led to it.

A BRIEF DISCUSSION OF COPYRIGHT

It's Your Book ... Right?

DISCLAIMER

While I did plenty of homework while composing this chapter and consulted with an attorney for general feedback, these measures are not tantamount to a law degree or a specialization in publishing copyright law (I have neither.)

This chapter is meant to get you thinking. It is not a replacement for legal advice. Consult a copyright attorney if you have any specific concerns, specifically as it relates to work-for-hire language.

In chapter zero, we discussed the truths of hiring a book designer. The first truth spoke to the notion that you are investing in a process, not a product.

That said, there *is* a product that results from the process you're investing in, and it's important you understand exactly what it is. That product is the final design. This design might be conveyed to you via a few print-ready PDFs, an EPUB file, and whatever other files you absolutely need to get the book published.

What about the design files used to create the cover? What about the fonts, images, and other assets that comprise the cover? Surely, the *copyright* is yours, right?

Unless the terms of your agreement with the designer specifically stipulate to your ownership of these materials as a work made for hire, your designer or publisher retains ownership. This includes the design's copyright. Of course, this doesn't include the copyright of the *book* itself. But if the design was created by a freelance designer or a publishing firm, and there was no language in your agreement declaring the ownership of the copyright and ownership of design files, it all defaults to them.

Intuitively, it may seem like you should have ownership over every piece of the project. But if you transpose that thinking to other services, the logic starts to fall apart. Imagine you stop into your local coffee shop for a latte. You watch the barista clink and clank and steam and pour until, voila, a delicious beverage appears in front of you. Imagine then saying, "I'll need the ingredients, the steamer, and the recipe, just in case I want to make it again."

It would be unreasonable to assume you're entitled to any of that. Just like that barista, your designer is a skilled technician, creating your product with tools. Just like your coffee shop has invested in equipment, ingredients, and inventory, your designer has invested in hardware, software, and assets.

"That's a stretch," you may be thinking. "After all, can't the designer simply copy and paste the files at no cost to them?"

Yes, and from my perspective, this is actually a reason to be *more* protective of my assets. I've put years of expertise and analysis into crafting sophisticated design templates in an effort to improve my value among the competition. As easy as those templates are to copy and share—compared to, say, a milk steamer—it behooves me to keep them close to my vest.

Another issue with simply zipping the project files over to you is that it potentially presents legal issues. Your designer purchases licenses for the fonts and stock assets they use to create your design, and these licenses may not be transferable, which may limit the designer's ability to provide these assets to authors or other designers.

> **Zipping project files over to you potentially presents legal issues. Licenses for fonts and stock assets may not be transferable.**

While it may not be intuitive to the average author, your designer has plenty of reasons to be protective of their source files. That said, you will almost certainly encounter designers who are willing to share them without a second thought. Perhaps you already have. Aside from the legal implications pertaining to licensed assets, it's really just a value judgment by the designer. Acknowledging my bias, I'd argue that if a designer chooses not to share their files and is under no contractual obligation to do so, it's a reasonable stance.

Acquiring the Source Files the Right Way

Let's assume you've accepted that you aren't automatically entitled to the source files. However, you still deem it important to have access to them. You may even have a cursory knowledge of design software, or perhaps you just view it as a safety measure to archive your book files.

Start off by having the conversation. Again, some designers will zip the files over, no questions asked. Others will consider it a deliverable that is outside the scope of a standard book design agreement. If that's the case, find out what it might take for your designer to adjust their contract language such that you receive the files and copyright ownership once the project is complete.

As with all things design, there is no set standard, so you'll have to work out a reasonable rate with your designer. And remember that they may not be able to provide you with licensed fonts and stock imagery used to compose your artwork. You'll likely need to invest in those assets separately.

Do You Actually Need the Files?

Perhaps you read the previous section and thought, *Gosh, I have to spend* more *on this project? When will it end?* If you had this reaction, I'd encourage you to consider whether you actually need the files.

Let's say you *do* acquire the source files. Then, a month or a year or five years later you decide it's time to edit the book. One of three things happens:

1. **You'll try to do it yourself.** Even if you already have the software to do it, how adept are you at operating it? Are you confident you'll be able to crack the files open and edit them without disrupting the structure of the document? Will you have to purchase fonts and stock images to ensure the file works? Will you know exactly how to export the files? And even if you accomplish all

of this, what was the opportunity cost of doing it yourself versus paying a designer?

2. **You'll pay a cheaper designer to edit the files.** You're glad you hired the all-star to handle the larger project, but surely a junior designer with a much lower hourly rate can manage updates, right? Putting aside the concept of "you get what you pay for": Once you've already paid your original designer for the files, are you gaining value on balance by hiring a cheaper resource? Consider that this young gun will have to familiarize themselves with the files, ramp up on the project in general, and could encounter any number of issues in file preparation if they aren't well-versed in the world of publishing prepress. Why not skip the headache and stick with your ringer?

3. **You'll pay your original designer to edit the files.** Whether or not you have acquired your design files, this is the smartest play. No one is more well equipped to edit a file than the person who created it—assuming your original designer is someone you'd like to work with again.[40]

I will close this section by recognizing that there *is* value to archiving your design files. What if your original designer becomes nonresponsive or unavailable for any reason? Even if you fully plan to stick with your primary designer, it may help you sleep at night to know the files are safely stored on your own hard drive. It's tantamount to insurance.

It's completely reasonable to think in those terms. So I ask you: When was the last time you were insured for free?

---

40 And of course they are. You read this book and made an excellent design hire!

Have the Conversation

The purpose of this book is to better equip you to navigate the book design process of your publishing journey. Understanding copyright and ownership is just another part of that bigger picture.

If you desire to have access to your files and/or own the copyright to the cover, let your designer know in advance of the collaboration. They may be willing to negotiate a fair price point for the transfer of both and include it in their proposal and project agreement. Others might put up no defense at all and will happily transfer everything to you when the project's complete. However they approach it, you can factor it into how you perceive the value of that relationship.

> **If you desire to have access to your files and/or own the copyright to the cover, let your designer know in advance of the collaboration.**

DESIGN DEBRIEF!
CHAPTER 8: A BRIEF DISCUSSION OF COPYRIGHT

Understand Your Agreements

When hiring your designer, get an understanding of
the parameters of the collaboration. What are the final
deliverables? What are you and aren't you entitled to?

Design Work Is Intellectual Property Too

Designers also retain rights to their original creations
unless otherwise negotiated. Final, prepared
design files are typically what you "own."

When in Doubt, Ask an Attorney

Copyright law is complicated. If anything's unclear—especially
with images, fonts, or shared content—consult legal help.

AI AND DESIGN COLLABORATIONS
Do Book Designers Still Belong?

The onset of AI has touched virtually every profession to some degree. Few industries are as prone to its impacts as publishing. Content creation is a large part of publishing, from ghostwriting to design, and portions of each of these processes can be supercharged by AI. This portends a shift in the definition of publishing services and the roles that administer them.

As a designer, I am occasionally asked about my concerns regarding my own long-term viability. Is my livelihood in danger? Can the skills I've spent years refining be completely undermined by a generative AI platform that can replicate the work I do?

I've long held that it would be hubristic to shrug off AI as a complete nonthreat to what I do, because I can't really conceive of its capabilities five or ten years from now. But as of this writing, I view it as a welcome tool, invaluable both for idea generation and for mitigating certain irritating tasks which, ten years ago, I longed for a workaround.

In fact, AI has been a part of graphic design for years. While generative AI is the new frontier, the concept of digital functionalities replacing manual tasks is nothing new. Consider that graphic artists of yesteryear were not only conceiving the creative solutions but were also physically cutting, pasting, coloring, and using other manual craft techniques to manipulate images. No longer. Modern graphic design is a product of technological advances that rendered those techniques obsolete. Almost overnight, old-school designers had to learn how to manage this software to stay viable. The ability to draw or craft by hand was no longer a prerequisite. Just like that, an entire vocation was redefined.

I think the impact of modern AI will be similar. I don't think my market value will be fully evaporated by AI anytime soon; however, if I don't embrace it, I will be displaced by those who are leveraging it as a tool to better serve the market.

How AI Can Benefit Your Project

As with just about any modern task, book design collaborations can be enhanced by AI. Embracing these applications can streamline the flow of ideas between you and your designer. It's understandable that authors at times have difficulty expressing ideas to designers, and at times the reverse can be true. Each of the applications I discuss in this section mitigates that concern in some way, encouraging clarity of communication.

Concept Mock-ups

The most visible way generative AI has seeped into my process is by way of clients supplying me with AI-generated concepts.

"I asked [AI of choice] to generate some book covers based on my title and a book description, and here's what it came up with."

I welcome this exercise for one primary reason: it helps the author show what they struggle to tell. Many authors are not visually inclined and have difficulty expressing the vision that exists in their mind's eye. If an AI mock-up can help convey their vision, it removes a common and frustrating roadblock.

Of course, these mock-ups are not tantamount to usable solutions. The text is usually scrambled, and all manner of glitchy artifacts litter the design. They are purely proofs of concept, which can be used as inspiration for the designer.

> **AI mockups are not tantamount to usable solutions. They are proofs of concept, which can be used as inspiration for the designer.**

It would be reasonable to wonder, *Doesn't this make the designer's job significantly easier?* Speaking from my own experience, the answer is: *not enough to matter.* As noted, generative AI can optimize the communication of vision, but the heaviest lifts of the process still rest with the designer. What it does do is strip away some of the grunt work to allow the designer to be more efficient with their creative energy.

It's important to note that AI prompts don't tell the whole story. In some cases, it can be confining for a designer to work off direction that comprises specific examples. As such, it's important to remain open to design solutions beyond those that were suggested by a generative AI.

DESIGNECDOTE:
Win One for the Humans!

I worked with an author who supplied six AI-generated cover mock-ups. "This is definitely the direction I'd like to go," she added. The mock-ups had all been generated from the same prompt and, as such, were relatively similar solutions. I dropped them into my inspiration board and set into ideating.

I developed a suite of concepts that were generally in line with the provided direction. As a creative exercise, I then developed a unique concept that had little to do with the provided direction. But it was a solution I thought might serve the author's message.

Lo and behold, she leapt at the unique concept. The AI mock-ups went by the wayside.

Do I share this to make light of my creative prowess? No.[41] Or to rub AI's digital schnoz in it? No.[42] I share it to remind you that AI mock-ups are merely a reflection of your inputs. Sure, you can provide multiple prompts and get different results. But don't reduce your book designer's value to that of a skilled mimic. You might just miss out on the cover of your dreams.

Visual Assets

Stock assets have long been part of the modern graphic designer's arsenal. Vast libraries of licensable visuals like photographs, vector graphics, and icons, created and provided by artists the

---

41 Yes.

42 Also yes.

world over, are used by graphic designers as building blocks for their unique designs.

Many stock asset platforms are now providing AI-generated content, or even feature their own generative AI tools. Let's say a client requests a graphic of a golden retriever wearing a football helmet, riding a blue horse with a rainbow tail, leaping over a green pickup truck.[43] Prior to generative AI, I'd have to gather a few different stock images and spend considerable time in Photoshop creating a composite image. Today, it's possible I could pop that prompt into a generative AI and get something fairly close to the mark.

As with the cover mock-ups, the results are not final solutions. Any designer using them as such is taking a major shortcut. But the results are typically satisfactory, to the degree that I save front-end time and effort which I'd sooner appropriate toward ensuring the final product is better than it has to be. To me, that's where the true promise of AI reveals itself. The designer spends less time and energy on the repetitive, annoying tasks. This equates to more focus on the creative process and fine-tuning.

The elephant in the room is the ethical question of AI generating assets that are based on original creations. This is a murky debate with far-reaching legal and ethical implications; as such, it is one that warrants a much broader discussion than this chapter is equipped to delve into. If you're concerned about these matters, have the discussion with your designer and arrive at a path forward.

Brainstorming

File this under "AI fast-tracking the annoying parts of the process." We think of brainstorming as a helpful exercise, but it rarely reveals

---

43 Believe it or not, I've received far stranger requests.

a final solution and often may limit ideation.[44] The process we have come to accept is "brainstorm, screen, iterate, refine, execute." In other words: think of a bunch of stuff, pluck the best ideas, consider them from all angles to reveal more creative solutions, fine-tune an approach, and ultimately move forward with it. By supporting that initial stage with an AI, you've not only simplified the most demanding step but created inspiring momentum. This will heat the coals under the rest of the process.

On and On and On ...

I could fill another book with ways AI can be meaningfully applied to the design process, but that's not why I wrote this chapter.[45] My goal with this section is to help authors understand that designers using AI functionalities aren't pushing a button and generating your book. Not hardly.

The most forward-thinking designers are leveraging it as a tool that can supercharge a collaboration. They're already using AI in the ways I outlined and many more. Maybe someday an AI will be so sophisticated that it can fully replace a human book designer, executing without flaw the *thousands* of major and minor inputs, decisions, and midstream adaptations that weave together to form a successful book design project. Until then, count on your designer to leverage AI to whatever degree you are comfortable. And if that is "not at all," so be it.

44 Adam Grant. "Why Brainstorming Doesn't Work," *Time*. October 24, 2023. https://time.com/6327515/brainstorming-doesnt-work-essay/

45 Yes, I wrote it, not AI!

DESIGN DEBRIEF!
CHAPTER 9: AI AND DESIGN COLLABORATIONS

AI as a Tool

While AI can't yet replace the nuance and adaptability of a skilled book designer, it's an increasingly valuable aid— particularly for idea generation and automating repetitive tasks. Designers who embrace AI will have a competitive edge.

Concept Mock-ups Spark Collaboration

AI-generated mock-ups can help authors visually communicate ideas they struggle to describe. These aren't final designs, but they can inspire productive direction-setting between author and designer.

Designers Add Value beyond AI

Even when AI gives a strong visual start, the designer's expertise in message, strategy, and execution is still what turns mock-ups into powerful, professional covers. AI shows options—designers create solutions.

AI Enhances Visual Asset Creation

Generative AI can quickly produce complex or whimsical imagery that might otherwise take hours to build from stock photos. This saves time on technical grunt work and frees designers to focus on creativity and polish.

Strategic Brainstorming and Efficiency

AI can kickstart brainstorming by offering a wide range of visual ideas instantly. This accelerates momentum and helps focus the designer's energy on refining and executing the best direction.

ALL YOU REALLY NEED TO KNOW

I've got a dirty secret to tell you. And I'll only share it now, after you've powered through all ten chapters.

The entirety of this book could have been whittled into a lone string of advice that I have evoked repeatedly throughout the course of this manuscript:

Hire the right designer, and the rest will take care of itself.

I reprise this statement—hyperbolic as it is—to drive home the point I'm trying to make: identifying the best design resource *for you* is the single most important driver of ensuring a successful outcome. This applies to any form of design you may need to commission, but I think it's especially important in publishing.

My hope is this book will help you identify the characteristics that define "the best designer for you." It can be tempting to limit your focus to common factors like availability, rates, and portfolio appeal. And that's fine to an extent, because they do matter. But they simply don't paint the full picture of any given design resource.

Once you've pooled a few candidates who objectively fit the bill, you must ask yourself two important questions:

1. How do *you* define a successful collaboration?[46]

2. How does each of your book design candidates align with that definition?

The first answer will vary from author to author because it is a function of what a given individual deems important. For example, I've had potential clients tell me up front, "I don't need a perfect book, but I do need this project done in three weeks." A successful project in that person's eyes will look very different from that of someone who'd rather be meticulous and take the time they need to get it right.

Once you've answered that first question, you can use it as a basis for evaluating the second question. How will your potential designer plug into your ideal project flow?

Wheat and Chaff

Remember what we learned in chapter 4: *anyone* can be a graphic designer. They don't need a credential of any kind. And there is no standardization across providers. Because of this, the spectrum of talent and service quality in book design is as wide as the Grand Canyon. You've got dabblers charging bargain rates, you've got industry vets charging prestige prices. Scarier yet, you've got dabblers charging prestige prices.

This leads to whiplash in the marketplace. Consumers aren't getting a consistent pitch, because the service providers

---

46 Remember, I'm not just talking about the *product*. Think mostly about the *process*: that which occurs between hiring your designer and receiving your final files.

themselves are all over the place. Even more troubling, some so-called "high-end" resources might bloat their process to make their services *seem* more valuable in an effort to validate their eye-popping price tag. This is counterweighted by quick-fix resources touting a low-touch, transactional design relationship for next to nothing. The landscape of design services is rough, rocky, uneven, and full of pitfalls. It can be dizzying for the consumer.

The thing to remember is that in graphic design, as with any service, cost and value are two very different things. And given how difficult "value" can be to define in the world of graphic design, owing to that broad and uneven spectrum of talent and resources, you'll benefit from approaching your search in a thoughtful, informed manner. My hope is this book will help you do just that.

> **Given how difficult value can be to define in the world of design, you'll benefit from approaching your search in a thoughtful, informed manner.**

My final bit of guidance, coming as it does after more than thirty thousand words on the subject, rings a bit counterintuitive: *don't overthink it.*

You don't need to conduct a sweeping, months-long search for your perfect designer. Gather a handful of names via referrals and your own search efforts.[47]

Let me further simplify it for you.

---

47 You can even look on the copyright page of a book that you think is particularly well designed. Chances are the designer's name is listed. Look them up!

To find your designer, do this:

1. Read the first half of this book.[48]

2. Reach out to one or more designers you've found via trusted referrals and/or your own research.

3. Ask any you're interested in—be it one or several—to hop on a phone call or video conference. Get to know them, feel them out, and ask some questions about their process.

4. Make your decision with confidence.

5. Watch (and contribute!) as your book comes to life.

It's as simple as that.

The Real Estate Agent

In 2023, I bought a house. It was my first time going through the process, and I couldn't help but notice the parallels between a great buying agent and a great book designer. The stakes were high and the stress was constant as my wife and I viewed properties, made an offer, negotiated, collected documents, met with a lender, courted insurance providers, and on and on and on, dropping chunks of cash at every stop on the line. The whole process was stressful and anxiety-stoking.

But my real estate agent, Bradley, always lowered the temperature. He was always calm and unflashy. He was also deeply knowledgeable and highly experienced. He took the time to understand what we were after and geared our search accordingly. He had a thorough answer for my many, many questions. He

48 Read the second half to crush the collaboration!

was extremely accountable. He never shied away from providing counsel or putting a bit of pressure on the selling agent. He made the whole process, tailor-made as it was to trigger my anxieties, unfold in a smooth and oddly satisfying manner.

Bradley will be the first to tell you he's not the right agent for everyone, but he was a perfect fit for us. Thankfully, he was a personal friend whose background and style I was already comfortable with, but it strikes me that if I *hadn't* known him previously, I still would have used him. He made a complicated process—one that asked much of both of us—feel seamless because he understood where I was coming from and where I wanted to be. And together, we found a home that my family loves. I'm not sure where we would have been without him.

Now get out there and find a book designer who makes you feel the same way.

ACKNOWLEDGMENTS

I've typeset a zillion acknowledgments sections in my career, but until now I never realized how hard it is to write one. I'm going to do my best to keep this concise but, at the same time, will make no apologies for turning over as many stones as necessary.

To my family: My wife Sarah, my daughter Hazel, my parents Jason and Eileen, my brother John, my sisters-in-law Lucy and Amy, my in-laws Jim and Merrio, and my niece and nephew, Emma and John. I'm very fortunate to have you all in my life. You never make me feel foolish for putting myself out there.

To my extended family: Just because I don't see you often doesn't mean you didn't have a formative impact. A special nod to my uncle, the late Danny Shanahan, who inspired me to pursue a career as a creative professional.

To my friends: I won't name names here, because where does one draw the line? I'll just say that I'm lucky to have many, many friends who have impacted my perspective and shaped who I am over the years. Classmates, coworkers, music pals, neighborhood buddies, and beyond. Grateful for all of you.

To my career inspirations and business partners: At risk of forgetting someone, I *will* name names here because there is a core group of individuals who have made my career possible. I could write a page for each of you; instead, I will make a list that I hope captures the names (in no particular order) of those who inspired me to think better, work smarter, and continuously refine the path I'm on: Tammy Watkins, Van Kornegay, Lisa Sisk, Carl Jenkinson, Melissa Ligon, Lea Ann Kornegay, Al Fadhen, Kate Colbert, Amanda Rooker, Lanette Pottle, Jeremy Sutton, Adam Witty, Kim Hall, Patti Boysen, Eland Mann, John Myers, Justin Batt, F. Scott Feil, Jeremy Sutton, Jason Bell, Jenny Lisk, Jen Gingerich, Ian Koviak, Anthony Damaschino, Allison Trowbridge, Sandra Smith, Marty Fort, and whoever else has given me a vote of confidence in some way. Thanks for guiding me through, keeping me busy, and trusting me to put your best foot forward.

To the design team: One of the most fulfilling experiences of my life was leading a design team of funny, smart, talented, and hardworking friends. You made my days better and offered unflinching support when I decided to set off on my journey as a business owner. Thank you to Megan, Wes, Carly, Melanie, Jamie, Mary, Katie, Chris, and Steven—the design work and dad jokes you brought to the table were always second to none.

To my authors and design clients: Call it schmoozy to thank clients, but when you build a business from scratch, you develop a gratitude for the folks who invest in your livelihood. I'm lucky to say that there's no way I could name everyone, but to countless individuals for whom I've designed something across my career, thanks for the opportunity.

To my publishing team: Thanks once again to Eland Mann for his editorial insight; to Nate Best for dialing in the manuscript; to Lucy Morton for flagging 211 proofing edits (remember when I told you proofreads are important?); to Kate Colbert for her peerless publishing expertise and encouragement along the way; and David Diamond, Jenny Lisk, Anthony Damaschino, and Ian Koviak for providing invaluable manuscript feedback; and to Steve Spangler for your willingness to write a brilliant foreword and wholehearted support of this project.

To my cat, June Carter Cat: Thanks for the companionship as I wrote this book and built my business. Sorry we had to cut your tail off. A nub looks great on you.

ABOUT THE AUTHOR

George B. Stevens is a book designer and musician. Born and raised in Charleston, South Carolina, he developed an interest in creating at a young age, always sketching, writing, and noodling on instruments before he had much (or any) capability for doing so. He found his creative footing in high school, serving as the editor-in-chief of the newspaper and learning his first song on guitar on December 25, 1999. It was "When the Saints Go Marching In."

A magna cum laude graduate of the University of South Carolina, he earned a bachelor's degree in journalism with a focus in visual communications. He began his career as a book designer in 2007 at a publishing startup in his hometown of Charleston. For the next twelve years, he designed hundreds of books, eventually serving as creative director to a plucky and lovable design team, overseeing the development of book designs for authors all over the world. In 2019, George exited his full-time role to found G Sharp Design, LLC, a graphic design practice mainly serving nonfiction authors and publishing professionals.

George is also a busy musician, performing steadily as a guitarist, vocalist, and mandolin player in and around the Charleston area. His musical adventures have taken him to stages at major festivals and venues like Merlefest, Floydfest, and the Charleston Bluegrass Festival. In addition to music, he is a passionate runner, having completed three marathons and more than a dozen half-marathons.

George is married to Sarah, whose sweet, encouraging demeanor and "go for it!" attitude gave him the confidence to start his business, build his music career, and write this book. Together they have a beautiful daughter, Hazel, and a rascally nub-tailed cat named June. They live in North Charleston, South Carolina.

GO BEYOND THE BOOK

George B. Stevens is a book designer, entrepreneur, and thought leader whose professional mission is to make self-publishing look better.

To reach out about **podcast appearances, guest contributions,** and **speaking opportunities**—or simply to say hello—send him an email:

❚ george@gsharpmajor.com

To learn more about George, his book design practice, and the ways he is tirelessly advancing his professional mission, visit his website:

❚ www.gsharpmajor.com

To connect with George on social media:

❚ facebook.com/gsharpdesign
instagram.com/gsharpdesign
linkedin.com/georgestevensdesign